1 MON'
FREE
READING

at
www.ForgottenBooks.com

By purchasing this book you are eligible for one month membership to ForgottenBooks.com, giving you unlimited access to our entire collection of over 1,000,000 titles via our web site and mobile apps.

To claim your free month visit:

www.forgottenbooks.com/free1279780

ISBN 978-0-364-86409-8
PIBN 11279780

❋ MINUTES ❋

— OF THE —

LOUISIANA ANNUAL CONFERENCE,

Methodist Episcopal Church, South.

Forty-Ninth Session,

LOUISIANA AVENUE CHURCH, New Orleans, La.

DECEMBER 5-10, 1894.

Bishop JOHN C. GRANBERY, D. D., - - - - - President.
Rev. JOHN T. SAWYER, - - - - - - - - Secretary.
Rev. FITZGERALD SALE PARKER, - - - Asst. Secretary.
Rev. WILLIAM G. EVANS, - - - - - Asst. Secretary.
Rev. HENRY H. AHRENS, - - - - - - Asst. Secretary.

NEW ORLEANS:
Hopkins' Printing Office, 22 Commercial Place.

MINUTES

— OF THE —

LOUISIANA ANNUAL CONFERENCE,

Methodist Episcopal Church, South.

FORTY-NINTH SESSION,

Louisiana Avenue Church, New Orleans, La.

December * 5-10, * 1894 *

Bishop JOHN C. GRANBERY, D. D., - - - - - President.
Rev. JOHN T. SAWYER, - - - - - - - - Secretary.
Rev. FITZGERALD SALE PARKER, - - - Asst. Secretary.
Rev. WILLIAM G. EVANS, - - - - - Asst. Secretary.
Rev. HENRY H. AHRENS, - - - - - - Asst. Secretary.

NEW ORLEANS:

Hopkins' Printing Office, 22 Commercial Place.

BISHOP JOHN C. GRANBERY, D. D.

ᖶouisiana ᴀnnual ᴄonference.

MINUTES.

The Forty-ninth Session of the Louisiana Annual Conference of the Methodist Episcopal Church, South, was held in the Louisiana Avenue M. Ep. Ch., South, in New Orleans, La., beginning Wednesday, December 5, 1894, and adjourning on Monday, December 10, 1894, Bishop John C. Granbery, D. D., in the chair.

The daily sessions were held from 9:30 A. M., to 1:30 P. M., and were opened with devotional exercises by Bishop Granbery and various members of the Conference.

John T. Sawyer was elected Secretary and Fitzgerald S. Parker, William G. Evans and Henry H. Ahrens, Assistant Secretaries.

The following answered to roll call during the session:

Clerical—James L. Wright, John A. Miller, B. F. White, Thos. H. McClendon, Thos. J. Upton, John F. Wynn, Henry O. White, Charles W. Carter, Marcus C. Manly, Robert Parvin, Robert A. Davis, Robert Randle, George Jackson, John M. Brown, Thomas S. Randle, Jacob D. Harper, Robert S. Isbell, Felix G. Hocutt, John T. Sawyer, Joseph B. Walker, John M. Johnston, N. S. Cornell, Lewis A. Reed, James A. Parker, J. F. Patterson, T. K. Faunt Le Roy, John B. Cassity, Samuel S. Keener, John L. P. Sheppard, James M. Beard, R. M. Blocker, Charles T. Munholland, Reuben S. Colier, Samuel H. Whatley, Robert J. Harp, F. D. Van Valkenburgh, Stephen J. Davies, J. B. A. Ahrens, H. J Boltz, Wilson Moore, J. F. Scurlock, James Ivy Hoffpauir, Franklin N. Parker, J. S. Sanders, Henry S. Johns, Houston Armstrong, J O. Bennett, Robert P. Howell, Willinm H. Hill, Harry W. May, George A. Mandeville, Fitzgerald Sale Parker, Christian Keener, William J. Porter, John B. Williams, Clayton Marcy Lyons, William F. Henderson, James E. Densen, John F. Foster, Charles F. Staples, James J. Kelly, Wm. H. La Prade, James L. Pierce Henry H. Ahrens, Isaac T. Reames, William G. Evans, William Schuble, E. L. Singeltary, J. White Davis, James M. Henry, William Winans Drake, Herman W. Knickerbocker, Benjamin H. Sheppard, H. Milton Banks, James Russell Roy, John B. Kent, William D. Gaskins, M G. Jenkins. Berry T. Crews, P. A. Johnston, Hiram R. Singleton, J. T. Leggett, R. M. Tucker, V. D. Skipper, G. D. Anders, W. L. Linfield, J. P. Haney, N. J. Roberts, Paul M. Brown, W. M. Sullivan. Robt. B. Downer. Albert S. Lutz. Robert H. Wynn, Lyman F. Jackson, Noel B. Norwood, Wm. T. Currie, E. T. Densen, C. R. Seward, W. A. Clarke, Robt. C. Grace, W. B. Van Valkenburgh, A. W. Turner, J. W. Lee, H. W. Rickey, Elton Wilson, R. R. Randle, T. M. Wafer, Williams E. Akin, W. T. Woodward, G. P. White, W. H. Benton, S. B. Beall, T. A. Luster; and

Lay—David Zable, W. B. Thomson, C. L. Andrews, E. P. Mackie, S. B. McCutchen, Rev. John Franklin, W. G. Wadley, J. W. Taylor, H. H. White, H. G. Goodwyn, J. B. Pickles, J. T. Baker. Dr. A. S. Helmick, Samuel Whited, John N. Pharr, A. M. Mayo, Hon. H. C. Newsom, Col. I. D. Wall, A. N. Brown; L. G. Gowers.

Question 1. Who are admitted on trial? Albert S. J. Neill, Robert W. Vaughan, James Jesse Smylie, Robert W. Randle, Charles C. Miller, W. D. Pickens, Ira Lincoln Bronson, Earl Leslie Alford, Wiley Griffin Roberts, Louis E. Wicht.

Question 2. Who remain on trial? John W. Lee, Harry W. Rickey, Elton Wilson, Williams E. Akin, W. T. Woodward, George P. White, W. H. Benton, Tatum M. Wafer, S. B. Beall, N. E. Joyner, R. R. Fandle, W. B. Van Valkenburgh, A. W. Turner, Talbot A. Luster, Willie A. Clarke, Robert C. Grace, Chester R. Seward, E. J. Densen.

Question 3. Who are discontinued? John Herbert Stafford, at his own request.

Question 4. Who are admitted into full connection? Albert S. Lutz, Robert H. Wynn, Lyman F. Jackson, Noel B. Norwood, William T. Currie.

Question 5. Who are re-admitted? None.

Question 6. Who are received by transfer from other Conferences? R. W. Tucker, R. S. Gale, H. R. Singleton, V. D. Skipper, J. T. Leggett, W. L. Linfield, G. P. White, W. T. Woodward, Wm. T. Currie, W. M. Sullivan, W. H. Benton, Geo. D. Anders, Paul M. Brown, Nathan J. Roberts, R. B. Downer, S. B. Beall, T. A. Luster, J. P. Haney, P. A. Johnston, from the Mississippi Conference and E. N. Evans from the Little Rock Conference.

Question 7. Who are the deacons of one year? Samuel S. Bogan, John B. Kent, B. H. Sheppard, W. D. Gaskins, W. M. Sullivan, J. T. Leggett, J. P. Haney, Paul M. Brown, James R. Roy.

Question 8. What traveling preachers are elected deacons? Albert S. Lutz, Lyman F. Jackson, William T. Currie.

Question 9. What traveling preachers are ordained deacons? Albert S. Lutz, Lyman F. Jackson, William T. Currie.

Question 10. What local preachers are elected deacons? William Winfree Buford, Albert S. J. Neill, James Erwin, Thomas Carter, Samuel B. Beall, William Honer Benton, James J. Smylie.

Question 11. What local preachers are ordained deacons? William W. Buford, Albert S. J. Neill, Thomas Carter, Samuel B. Beall, Wm. H. Benton, James J. Smylie.

Question 12. What traveling preachers are elected elders? Henry M. Banks, Herman W. Knickerbocker.

Question 13. What traveling preachers are ordained elders? Henry M. Banks, Herman W. Knickerbocker.

Question 14. What local preachers are elected elders? Frederick Mathies.

Question 15. What local preachers are ordained elders? None.

Question 16. Who are located this year? George A. Mandeville, at his own request; and W. F. Sanders and Charles E. McDonald.

Question 17. Who are supernumerary? Christian Keener.

Question 18. Who are superannuated? P. H. Diffenweirth, James L. Wright, Jesse Fulton, E. W. Yancey, George Jackson, Joseph H. Stone, Reynolds S. Trippett, Enos B. Foust, J. F. Scurlock, E. L. Singeltary, Thos. B. White.

Question 19. What preachers have died during the past year? A. M. Wailes.

Question 20. Are all the preachers blameless in their life and official administration? Their names were called, one by one, and their characters passed.

Question 21. What is the number of local preachers and members in the several circuits, stations, and missions of the Conference?

Local preachers.. 104
White members.. 27,990
Colored members 9

Total... 28,103

Question 22. How many infants have been baptized during the year? 1,291.

Question 23. How many adults have been baptized during the year? 1,022.

Question 24. What is the number of Epworth Leagues? 18.

Question 25. What is the number of Epworth League members? 700.

Question 26. What is the number of Sunday Schools? 290.

Question 27. What is the number of Sunday School teachers? 1835.

Question 28. What is the number of Sunday School scholars? 13,526.

Question 29. What amount is necessary for the superannuated preachers, and the widows and orphans of preachers? $4,900.

Question 30. What has been collected on the foregoing account, and how has it been applied? $3,293.23; and applied as follows:

Rev. P. H. Diffenweirth................ $105 00...taken by C. W. Carter.
"   J. H. Stone .... 105 00...taken by C. R. Seward.
"   Jesse Fulton..... .... 135 00...taken by R. S. Isbell.
"   E. W. Yancey...................... 130 00...taken by S. J. Davies.
"   George Jackson..... .... 138 00...taken by himself.
"   R. S. Trinpett...... .... 175 00...taken by J. T. Sawyer.
"   Enos B. Foust......... ... . 190 00...taken by J. S. Sanders.
"   James L. Wright........ .... 150 00...taken by himself.
"   J. M. Brown .... 145 00...taken by himself.
Mrs. J. W. Medlock............ .... 320 00...taken by J. B. Cassity.
"   R. R. Alexander.................... 100 00...taken by S B. McCutchen.
"   P. H. Goodwyn........ .... 120 00...taken by T. K. Faunt Le Roy
"   W. D. Stayton...................... 115 00...taken by W. H. Hill.
"   Jos. D. Adams.................... 120 00...taken by P. A. Johnston.
"   R. M. Crowson........ .... 95 00...taken by J. L. P. Sheppard.
"   W. Weimer.......................... 55 00...taken by H. O. White.
"   J. E. Bradley .... 95 00 .taken by A. M. Mayo.
"   J. J. Blonz .... 130 00...taken by H. H. Ahrens.
"   J. Lane Borden........ .... 180 00...taken by Jno. A. Miller.
"   G. M. Liverman........ .... 195 00...taken by Robert Randle.
Heirs of H. D. Kimball.......... ..... 40 09...taken by J. D. Harper.
Mrs. John Pipes .... 140 00...taken by Robt. J. Harp.
"   B. F. Alexander.................. 110 00...taken by Robert Randle.
Hanson Moss............................. 40 28 ..taken by H. O. White.
Mrs. Geo. Green........ .... 105 00...taken by J. B. Pickles.
Printing Minutes.................. ..... 60 00 ..taken by J. T. Sawyer.

$3,293 28

REPORT OF JOINT BOARD OF FINANCE.

RECEIPTS.

From Churches for Conference Claimants	$2836 03	
" New Orleans Depository	450 00	
" Colvin Fund	7 20	
For Bishops	693 38	
" Expenses of General Conference Delegates	121 95	
		$4,108 56

DISBURSEMENTS.

Paid Conference Claimants	$3233 23	
Remitted for Bishops	693 38	
" " General Conference Delegates	121 95	
Paid for Printing Minutes	60 00	
		$4,108 56

Ques. 31. What has been contributed for Missions?

William B. Thomson, Treasurer of the Board of Missions, made the following report, which was adopted, viz:

FOREIGN MISSIONS.

Dr.

	By Churches.	By Sunday Schools.	Totals.
New Orleans District	$1584 50	$418 91	$2003·41
Shreveport District	670 90	2 75	673 65
Opelousas District	637 20	27 15	664 85
Alexandria District	244 90		244 90
Arcadia District	633 90		633 90
Delhi District	425 40	7 00	432 40
	$4,196 80	$455 81	$4,652 61
Missionary Debt Collections			18 60
Anniversary Collection			47 50
			$4,718 71

Cr.

By Vouchers of T. B. Holt, Treasurer	$1436 75	
" " " " "	3186 07	
By cash on hand	95 89	
		$4,718 71

DOMESTIC MISSIONS.

Dr.

To Balance from last year	$ 19 91	
To Amounts collected from Churches	1561 65	
To Anniversary Collection	47 50	
		$1,629 06

Cr.

By Appropriations as follows:

New Orleans District...$270 00
Baton Rouge District...260 00
Opelousas District...260 00
Alexandria District..275 00
Shreveport District..315 00
Arcadia District,..65 00
Delhi District...120 00
Printing Minutes...60 C0
Balance on hand 4 06
                                                                                        $1,629 06

Total for Foreign Missions $4,718 71
Total for Domestic Missions 1,629 06

                    Grand Total $6,347 77

REPORT OF TREASURER OF WOMAN'S FOREIGN MISSIONARY SOCIETY OF THE LOUISIANA CONFERENCE, 1894.

New Orleans District:

Received from Louisiana Avenue Auxiliary..................$117 25
    "   " Felicity Street Auxiliary.............................91 10
    "   " Felicity Street Juvenile..............................8 35
    "   " Rayne Memorial Auxiliary.........................36 70
    "   " Rayne Memorial Juvenile...........................6 60
    "   " Baton Rouge Auxiliary................10 00—$270 00

Shreveport District:

Received from Shreveport Auxiliary.............................$ 70 25
    "   " Shreveport Juvenile...................................9 90
    "   " Mrs. Alexander, State Organizer.................24 25
    "   " Belle Bower Auxiliary................................8 35
    "   " Belle Bower Juvenile.................................12 41
    "   " Mansfield Auxiliary...................................29 50
    "   " Keatchie Auxiliary.....................................17 15
    "   " Keatchie Juvenile......................................20 40
    "   " Grand Cane Auxiliary................................18 64
    "   " Pleasant Hill Auxiliary...............................3 60
    "   " Marthaville Auxiliary..................................1 25
    "   " Pine Hill Auxiliary.....................................5 00
    "   " Pine Hill Juvenile......................................1 50
    "   " Mt. Zion Auxiliary...................1 50— 223 70

Delhi District:

Received from Oak Ridge Auxiliary............................$ 14 95
    "   " Lake Providence Auxiliary..........................6 10
    "   " Lake Providence Juvenile..............4 55— 25 60

Opelousas District:

Received from Opelousas Auxiliary.............................$ 26 40
    "   " Opelousas Juvenile....................................5 85
    "   " Lafayette Auxiliary....................................13 85
    "   " Lafayette Juvenile.....................................2 00
    "   " New Iberia Auxiliary.................................10 00
    "   " Randle Home Auxiliary..............................3 30
    "   " Crowley Auxiliary.......................36 05— 97 45

Alexandria District:
    Received from Lecompte Auxiliary......................................$ 14 70—   14 70

Arcadia District:
    Received from Ruston Auxiliary...$ 36 25
          "   " Ruston Juvenile....................................... 17 00
          "   " Homer Auxiliary................................... 14 00
          "   " Homer Juvenile... 2 40—   69 65

Baton Rouge District:
    Received from Amite City Auxiliary............................ $ 5 65—   5 65

Received from Mrs. R. S. Isbell 5 00

                 Total collected....................... . $711 75

                              MRS. S. B. McCUTCHEN, *Treasurer.*

SHREVEPORT, LA., Dec. 4, 1894.

    Ques. 32. What has been contributed for Church Extension?

    Rev. Fitzgerald Sale Parker, Treasurer of Board of Church Extension, made the following report, which was adopted, viz:

CHURCH EXTENSION.

Dr.

To Balance from last year... $ 8 95
To Amounts received on last year's collections....................   8 00
To Amounts received on this year's assessments:
    From New Orleans District.......................................$440 38
      " Shreveport   " 150 30
      " Opelousas   " 152 80
      " Alexandria   " 39 29
      " Arcadia   " 169 95
      " Delhi   "   .... 100 60— 1053 32
To Amount of Anniversary Collection.................................   113 99

                                      $1,184 26

Cr.

By Appropriation to Baton Rouge—S. S. Keener............ $ 75 00
       "   Shreveport—S. B. McCutchen............. 100 00
       "   Lacarine—J. M. Beard...................... 200 00
       "   Lafayette—T. S. Randle..................... 125 00—$ 500 00
       "   for printing Minutes—J. T. Sawyer........   60 00
       "   " Ch. Extension Bulletin—D. Morton...   15 00
By Current Expense, Drayage, &c   75
By Parent Board on account of 1894—Collections—D. Morton   500 00
By Balance Cash.. $ 77 51
         Vouchers .... 31 00— 108 51

                                      $1,184 26

REPORT OF TREASURER OF WOMAN'S PARSONAGE AND HOME
MISSION SOCIETY, LOUISIANA CONFERENCE, 1894.

To Balance from last year..		$ 92 13

To Receipts from Dues—

New Orleans District :

Received from Carondelet Auxiliary........... ....$	37 70	
" " Louisiana Avenue Auxiliary.................	33 15	
" " Rayne Memorial Auxiliary.............	29 90	
" " Rayne Memorial Juniors.................. ...	7 50	
" " Felicity Auxiliary...............	15 00	
" " Parker Chapel Auxiliary	14 30	
		$137 55

Opelousas District:

Received from Abbeville Auxiliary ....$	15 00	
" " Lafayette Auxiliary.............................	12 25	
" " Patterson Auxiliary.........................	10 05	
" " Lake Charles Auxiliary......	9 75	
" " Lake Charles Juniors.......................	4 00	
" " Opelousas Auxiliary	6 50	
" " Morgan City Auxiliary.	5 00	
" " Franklin Auxiliary.............	5 00	
" " Crowley Auxiliary.....	4 05	
		71 60

Arcadia District:

Received from Ruston Auxiliary...... .... $	14 50	
" " Minden Auxiliary.........	9 95	
" " Homer Juniors......	2 40	
		26 85

Delhi District:

Received from Tallulah Auxiliary..... ....$	17 75	
" " Oak Ridge Auxiliary..	13 00	
		30 75

Alexandria District:

Received from Lecompte Auxiliary ....$	5 55	
" " Alexandria Auxiliary................	4 45	
		10 00

Shreveport District :

Received from Shreveport Auxiliary........ ....$ 17 35—		17 35

Total Dues......	$294 10

RECEIPTS FROM WEEK OF PRAYER.

Received from Union Meeting held at Carondelet...............$	9 40	
" " " " " Rayne Memorial.......	12 44	
Offering from Louisiana Avenue Auxiliary.......................	5 35	
" " Parker Chapel Auxiliary...........	3 70	
" " Oak Ridge Auxiliary...............	2 40	
" " Felicity Auxiliary...............	1 00—	34 29

RECEIPTS FROM CARDS AND LINKS.

Received from Patterson Auxiliary........................ ....$	3 00	
" " Rayne Memorial Juniors...........	2 20—	5 20

RECEIPTS FROM SPECIAL DONATIONS.

Received for Parsonage at Abbeville..... ....$ 1 00—   1 00

RECEIPTS FROM DISTRICT MEETINGS.

Received from Meeting at Dryades Street Church... ....: $ 20 35
    "   "   "   " Rayne Memorial Church ...... ,...   9 10—   29 45

RECEIPTS FOR CITY MISSIONARY.

Received from Carondelet Street Auxiliary........... .... $ 31 15
    "   " Rayne Memorial Auxiliary ....,.,.........   30 00
    "   " Louisiana Avenue Auxiliary.......... ....   17 00
    "   " Felicity Street Auxiliary.. ....   15 00
    "   " Parker Chapel Auxiliary........... ....   12 00—   105 15

              Total receipts from all sources......... $561 32

DISBURSEMENTS.

Remitted to Mrs. Geo. P. Kendrick, General Treasurer,
    Dues of First Quarter..................... ,....... ..... $43 15
       " " Second   " 43 35
       " " Third   "   ....,.........,.,............ 23 80
       " " Fourth   " 31 70
                            $142 00
From Cards and Links ....·,......... ....   5 20
   " Special Collections................ ....   15 84
                            $163 04

Remitted to Rev. J. White Davis for Parsonage at Gilbert... ..$50 00
    "   "   " H. M. Banks "   "   " Dry Creek. 50 00
    "   "   " F. G. Hocutt "   ",   " West Lake. 50 00
    "   "   " J. J. Kelly   "   "   " Abbeville.. 50 00
                            200 00

Donation to Mrs. Wiley............... ....   20 00
Expenses—Circulars, P. O., Reports, Drafts, &c...................$13 25
Painting Sign for Tchoupitoulas Mission............ ....,... 5 00
                              18 25
Paid Miss Burbank, City Missionary (Salary).....................   90 00
         Balance on hand............... ....   70 03
                            $561 32

                     MRS. J. H. CAMPMAN,
                       Conference Treasurer.

New Orleans, La., December 4, 1894.

RECAPITULATION.

Amount raised by Conference Board...,............ ....$1,175 31
    "   "   " Woman's Parsonage and Home Mission Society...... 469 19

         Total for Church Extension.... ... . $1,644 50
         Total raised the previous year:............ .... 1,281 56

              Increase........ ....,........ $ 362 94

Ques. 33.   What has been done for the American Bible Society ? $344.25.

Ques. 34. What has been contributed for the support of presiding elders and preachers in charge?

Presiding Elders........... ....,...... ....$ 8,802.60
Preachers in Charge............. .... 52,060.35

$60,862.95

Ques. 35. What has been contributed for the support of Bishops? $311.38.

Ques. 36. What is the number of Societies, and estimated value of Church Edifices?

No. of Societies......... 345
No. of Church Edifices.. 296
Value of Church Edifices.................. ....$511,640.00

Ques. 37. What is the number of pastoral charges, and the number and value of parsonages owned by them?

No. of Charges................................:...................... 113
No. of Parsonages............................:................ 81
Value of Parsonages............. ....$81,337

Ques. 38. What is the number and value of district parsonages?

No. of District Parsonages........................ 3
Value of District Parsonages..... ....'......................$5000

Ques. 39. What are the educational statistics?

Education Fund $574.33
Paine & Lane Institute...................... .... 80.01

Ques. 40. Where shall the next session of the Conference be held? At Jackson, La.

Ques. 41. Where are the preachers stationed this year?

APPOINTMENTS.

NEW ORLEANS DISTRICT—(1) *John T. Sawyer, P. E.*

Carondelet Street........ ....(1) J. L. Pierce
Felicity Street........... ....(2) T. K. Faunt Le Roy
Rayne Memorial........................... ....(3) F. N. Parker
Louisiana Avenue......................... ....(1) C. M. Lyons
Moreau Street .... (1) J. M. Henry
Plaquemine and Donaldsonville............. .... (2) H. S. Johns
Carrollton Avenue..(1) L. A. Reed and C. Keener
Gretna and Craps Street............. ....(3) H. H. Ahrens
Parker Chapel...................... ....(3) R. H. Wynn
Algiers................. .... (1) J. B. Walker
Dryades Street....... . ...(2) F. S. Parker
Lower Coast Mission ....(2) N. B. Norwood
Covington.... ....(1) W. T. Currie
Talisheek .... (1) W. A. Clarke
Editor Familien Freund.................... .. ..J. B. A. Ahrens

BATON ROUGE DISTRICT.—(4) *P. A. Johnston, P. E.*

Baton Rouge..(3) S. S. Keener
Grossé Tete and False River...... ....(2) Wm. Schuble
East Baton Rouge...... ....(1) J. F. Wynn
Ascension Mission ...._..............(1) R. R. Randle
Live Oak.......................... ....(1) C. R. Seward
Port Vincent......... ....To be supplied by W. L. Hamil

Pontchatoula and Mission............(1) G. P. White and one to be supplied
Franklinton and Mission............(2) W. H. Benton and (1) W. G. Roberts
Amite City...(1) James J. Smylie
St. Helena......................................(3) Nathan J. Roberts
Pine Grove.......................................(2) J. P. Haney
East Feliciana..................................(4) Geo. D. Anders
Clinton...(1) S. B. Beall
Slaughter..(1) S. S. Bogan
Wilson...(4) R. W. Tucker
Zachary..(1) J. O. Bennett
Jackson..(3) H. R. Singleton
Bayou Sara.......................................(1) T. A. Luster
Centenary College.......................C. W. Carter, President
Centenary College.......................C. C. Miller, Professor
Centenary College.......................L. E. Witch, Student

OPELOUSAS DISTRICT.—(1) *H O. White, P. E*

Opelousas..(2) E. T. Densen
Washington.......................................(2) M. C. Manly
Plaquemine Brulée................................(2) J. S. Sanders
Prudhomme Circuit................................(1) S. H. Whatley
Lafayette..(2) T. S. Randle
Crowley..(3) W. W. Drake
Abbeville..(2) J. J. Kelly
New Iberia.......................................(1) J. M. Beard
Franklin...(2) Houston Armstrong
Jeannerette......................................(1) R. M. Blocker
Lake Charles.....................................(1) Robt. J. Harp
Jackson Street...................................(1) R. W. Randle
West Lake..(2) F. G. Hocutt
Pattersonville...................................(1) F. D. Van Valkenburgh
Morgan City......................................(1) James A. Parker
Sulphur Mine.....................................(1) W. D. Pickens
Grand Cheniére...................................(2) W. B. Van Valkenburgh
Indian Bayou.....................................(2) W. J. Porter
Lake Arthur......................................(1) R. P. Howell
Têche Circuit....................................(1) Albert S. J. Neill
Berwick..........................To be supplied by C. R. Montgomery
French Mission...................To be supplied by Joseph Berwick

ALEXANDRIA DISTRICT.—(8) *Stephen J. Davies, P. E.*

Alexandria.......................................(1) Lyman F. Jackson
Evergreen and Big Cane...........................(1) A. W. Turner
Lecompte and White Chapel........................(1) C. T. Munholland
Simsport...(1) W. T. Woodward
Melville and Bunkie..............................(1) J. E. Densen
Spring Creek.....................................(1) J. W. Lee
Glenmora Mission.................................(1) R. C. Grace
Dry Creek........................To be supplied by F. N. Sweeney
Montgomery.......................................(2) J. F. Patterson
Atlanta Circuit..................................(2) Wilson Moore
Centreville......................................(1) H. M. Banks
Columbia...(1) J. R. Roy
Boyce and Colfax.................................(1) J. I. Hoffpanir
Pineville..(1) J. M. Johnston
Bayou Chicot.....................................(2) J. B. Kent
Nugent Circuit...................................(1) Elton Wilson

SHREVEPORT DISTRICT.—(1) *J. L. P. Sheppard, P. E.*

Shreveport..(1) W. H. LaPrade
City Mission..(1) Albert S. Lutz
Mooringsport...(3) W. F. Henderson
Caddo..(1) Paul M. Brown
Mansfield..(2) B. T. Crews
Many...(1) J. M. Brown
Grand Cane...(1) W. H. Hill
Anacoco and S. Vernon.....................To be supplied by H. C. Murphy
Pleasant Hill..(1) J. B. Williams
Natchitoches Circuit.................................(1) H. W. Rickey
Coushatta..(1) J. E. Riddle
Wesley...(1) H. W. Wallace
South Bossier..(1) N. S. Cornell
North Bossier..(2) H. J. Boltz
Fort Jessup..(1) T. M. Boynton
De Soto..(2) S. S. Holliday
De Soto Mission...........................To be supplied by J. H. Johnson
Mansfield Female College.............................A. D. M'Voy, President
Vanderbilt University................................N. E. Joyner, Student

ARCADIA DISTRICT.—(1) *J. D. Harper, P. E.*

Homer..(1) V. D. Skipper
Haynesville..(2) R. S. Colier
Minden...(2) J. B. Cassity
Ringgold...(2) B. H. Sheppard
Bienville..(1) J. White Davis
Arcadia..(2) H. W. May
Summerfield..(1) Robert Randle
Ruston...(2) John A. Miller
Vienna...(1) R. W. Vaughan
Vernon...(1) C. F. Staples
Downsville...(2) D. C. Barr
Farmerville..(2) W. D. Gaskins
Valley...(1) Robt. Parvin
Lisbon...(1) Thos. J. Upton
Gannsville...(1) J. H. Brown

DELHI DISTRICT.—(1) *B. F. White, P. E.*

Monroe...(1) E. A. Evans
West Monroe..(3) W. G. Evans
Bastrop..(1) M. G. Jenkins
Lind Grove...(1) Thos. H. McClendon
Delhi..(2) John F. Foster
Floyd and Mission....................................(4) C. R. Godfrey
Lake Providence......................................(1) H. W. Knickerbocker
Oak Ridge..(2) Robert A. Davis
Harrisonburg...(1) Earl L. Alford
Waterproof...(1) Tatum M. Wafer
Winsboro...(1) Ira L. Bronson
Rayville...(4) Isaac T. Reames
Oakley and Vidalia...................................(1) Williams E. Akin
Calhoun and La Pine..................................(1) Robert S. Isbell

Transferred to the Mississippi Conference: W. M. Sullivan, J. T. Leggett, R. S. Gale, W. L. Linfield, R. B. Downer,

Superannuates: P. H. Diffenweirth, J. L. Wright, Jesse Fulton, E. W. Yancey, George Jackson, Joseph H. Stone, Reynolds S. Trippett, Enos B. Foust, J. F. Scurlock, E. L. Singeltary, Thos. B. White.

APPORTIONMENTS FOR 1895.

DISTRICTS.	Foreign Missions.	Domestic Missions.	Church Extension.	Conference Claimants.
New Orleans	$2350 00	$800 00	$593 75	$1005 00
Baton Rouge	1000 00	400 00	275 00	600 00
Opelousas	1100 00	450 00	283 75	660 00
Alexandria	600 00	250 00	212 50	410 00
Shreveport	1350 00	550 00	343 75	810 00
Arcadia	1350 00	550 00	343 75	705 00
Delhi	1250 00	400 00	322 50	710 00
	$9,000 00	$3,400 00	$2,375 00	$4,900 00

DISTRICTS.	Bishops.	Centenary and Mansfield Colleges.	General Board of Education.	Paine and Lane Inst.
New Orleans	$234 00	$234 00	$59 50	$40 00
Baton Rouge	145 00	145 00	27 50	30 00
Opelousas	148 00	148 00	28 00	20 00
Alexandria	100 00	100 00	21 50	20 00
Shreveport	193 00	193 00	34 50	35 00
Arcadia	160 00	160 0C	34 50	30 00
Delhi	154 00	154 00	32 00	25 00
	$1,134 00	$1,134 00	$237 50	$200 00

BOARDS AND COMMITTEES.

COMMITTEES OF EXAMINATION.

For Admission on Trial: T. K. Faunt Le Roy, W. H. LaPrade, J. A. Parker.

For First Year: F. S. Parker, G. D Anders, W. W. Drake.
For Second Year: F. N. Parker, J. L. Pierce, J. F. Foster.
For Third Year: V. D. Skipper, J. M. Henry, H. W. May.
For Fourth Year: J. B. A. Ahrens, R. W. Tucker, Stephen J. Davies.

UNDERGRADUATES.

First Year: Albert S. J. Neill, Robert W. Vaughan, James Jesse Smylie, Robert W. Randle, Charles C. Miller, W. D. Pickens, Ira Lincoln Bronson, Earl Leslie Alford, Wiley Griffin Roberts, Louis E. Wicht, N. E. Joyner, R. R. Randle, Geo. P. White, W. B. Van Valkenburgh, A. W. Turner.

Second Year: John W. Lee, Harry W. Rickey, Elton Wilson, Williams E. Akin, W. T. Woodward, W. H. Benton, Tatum M. Wafer, Samuel B. Beall, Willie A. Clarke, Chester R. Seward, R. C. Grace, E. T. Densen, Talbot A. Luster.

Third Year: Albert S. Lutz, Lyman F. Jackson, William T. Currie, Robert H. Wynn, Noel B. Norwood, Samuel S. Bogan, Paul M. Brown.

Fourth Year: John B. Kent, B. H. Sheppard, W. D. Gaskins, J. P. Haney, James R. Roy.

BOARD OF CHURCH EXTENSION.

Rev. John T. Sawyer, President; Rev. J. Ivy Hoffpauir, Secretary; Rev. Robert Randle, Treasurer; Revs. Thos. H. McClendon, Wm. F. Henderson, M. G. Jenkins, H. S. Johns. John B. Williams, N. J. Roberts; and Ed. P. Mackie, A. F. Jackson, H. C. Newsom, H. H. White, A. M. Mayo, J. W. Dawson, Dr. A. S. Helmick.

BOARD OF MISSIONS.

Rev. Jacob D. Harper, President; Rev. James A. Parker, Secretary; W. B. Thomson, Treasurer, Nos. 225 to 233 South Rampart Street, New Orleans, La.; Rev. James M. Beard, Robt. S. Isbell, H. W. Knickerbocker, Robt. A. Davis, Paul M. Brown; and Dr. W. D. White, Claiborne J. Foster, Isaac D. Wall, Dr. Robert Roberts, Jno. B. Pickles and Samuel Whited.

SUNDAY SCHOOL BOARD.

Rev. John F Foster, President; Revs. Thos. J. Upton, Henry H. Ahrens, N. S. Cornell, T. S. Randle, J. F. Patterson, William Schuble, Chas. T. Munholland; and Dr. J. W. Adams, E. E. Riggs, H. G. Goodwyn, A. M. Mayo.

BOARD OF EDUCATION.

Rev. W. H. La Prade, President; Revs. H. R. Singleton, C. W. Carter, W. W. Drake, F. G. Hocutt, J. L. Pierce, J. L. P. Sheppard, F. N. Parker, J. B. Cassity, John A. Miller, J. M. Johnston; and H. C, Newsom, A. H Gay, S. B. McCutchen, Dr. A S. Helmick, J. N. Pharr, E. G. Hunter, W. W.Carré.

BOARD OF COLPORTAGE.

Rev. Robt Parvin, President; Revs. F. D. V. n Valkenburgh, Chas. F. Staples, R. M. Blocker, J. S. Sanders, Houston Armstrong, Sam'l H. Whatley; and U. T. Blacksher, Daniel Brewer, G. L. P. Wren, David Zable, B. C, Lee, A N. Brown.

JOINT BOARD OF FINANCE.

	Clerical.	*Lay.*
New Orleans District	T. K. Faunt Le Roy,	David Zable,
Baton Rouge District	Samuel S. Keener,	L. J. Gowers,
Opelousas District	R. M. Blocker,	U T. Blacksher,
Alexandria District	J. Ivy Hoffpauir,	H. G. Goodwyn,
Shreveport District	W. H. La Prade,	S. B. McCutchen,
Arcadia District	Robert Randle,	J. W. Dawson,
Delhi District	M. G. Jenkins.	A. S. Helmick, M. D.

CHAIRMEN OF COMMITTEES FOR 1895.

Temperance—Rev. J. B. Walker.
Bible Cause—Rev. C. Marcy Lyons.
Church Publications—Rev. B. F. White.

VISITING COMMITTEES.

For Centenary College—Rev. J. O. Bennett, Lyman F. Jackson and E. N. Evans.
For Mansfield Female College—Rev. V. D. Skipper, W. H. LaPrade and J. M. Brown.

COMMITTEE ON CONFERENCE RELATIONS.

Rev. J. D. Harper, chairman; Revs. Isaac-T. Reames, Houston Armstrong, Geo. D. Anders, James I. Hoffpauir, T. K. Faunt Le Roy, Wm. F. Henderson.

COMMITTEE ON CHURCH PUBLICATIONS.

Rev. J. L. Pierce, chairman; Revs. J. B. Walker and R. W. Tucker.

COMMITTEE ON TEMPERANCE.

Rev. C. M. Lyons, chairman; Revs. Thos. J. Upton and Reuben S. Colier.

COMMITTEE ON BIBLE CAUSE.

Rev. F. N. Parker, chairman; Rev. R. M. Blocker and Hon H. C. Newsom.

COMMITTEE ON DISTRICT CONFERENCE RECORDS.

Rev. N. S. Cornell, chairman; Rev. W. Winans Drake and H H. White.

COMMITTEE ON PUBLIC WORSHIP.

Rev. John T. Sawyer, chairman; Rev. T. K. Faunt Le Roy and W. B. Thomson.

COMMITTEE ON MEMOIRS.

Rev. James A. Parker.

COMMITTEE ON NOMINATION OF BOARDS AND COMMITTEES.

Rev. Samuel S. Keener, chairman; Revs. Robert Randle, John A. Miller, J. S. Sanders, B. F. White, J. E. Densen, V. D. Skipper.

BOARD OF MANAGERS OF MANSFIELD FEMALE COLLEGE.

Rev. J. L. P. Sheppard, President; Revs. B. T. Crews and W. H. La Prade; and L B. Wilcox and A. F. Jackson.

BOARD OF MANAGERS OF PIERCE AND PAINE COLLEGE.

Rev. J. L. P. Sheppard, President; Rev. J. B. Williams and H. J. Davis, W. H. Jordan, W. C. Davis, W. T. Hopkins and J. J. Fike.

BOARD OF TRUSTEES OF ALEXANDRIA HIGH SCHOOL,

Hon. E. G. Hunter, Revs. J. I. Hoffpauir, R. Randle, John F. Wynn; and Wm. Hill, N. L. McGinnis and H. H. White.

BOARD OF TRUSTEES FOR WELCH & MARYE PROPERTY

Revs. T. K. Faunt Le Roy and J. I. Hoffpauir.

WOMAN'S PARSONAGE AND HOME MISSION SOCIETY OF THE LOUISIANA CONFERENCE.

President ....Mrs. F. A. Lyons, 4810 St. Charles Ave.
First Vice President..........................Mrs. John T. Sawyer, 3333 Magazine St.
Second Vice President .... Mrs. W. H. LaPrade, Shreveport, La.
Third Vice President........ Mrs. Warren C. Black, Second St. near Baronne.
Fourth Vice President............Mrs Linus Parker, Calhoun Ave cor. Jennet.
Fifth Vice President................. .... Mrs. Robert Randle, Shiloh, La.
Corresponding Secretary.............Mrs. Florence E. Russ, 3502 Camp St.
Recording Secretary ....Mrs. C. W. Carter, Jackson, La.
Treasurer..... .... .Mrs. J. H. Campman, Eighth St. near Camp.
Solicitor for "Our Homes,"..Miss Mary, Werlein, St. Charles & Nashville Aves.
State Organizer........... "   "   "   "   "   "

DISTRICT SECRETARIES.

New Orleans District—Miss Lizzie Wasson, Webster St. near Hurst.
Baton Rouge District————————— ————— —————
Opelousas District——————— ——. ———— ——
Alexandria District—Mrs. S. J. Davies, Alexandria, La.
Shreveport District- ———— ————
Arcadia District—Mrs. A. K. Klingman, Homer, La.
Delhi District—————— —— ————— ——— ———— — —

WOMAN'S FOREIGN MISSIONARY SOCIETY OF THE LOUISIANA
CONFERENCE.

President...........................Mrs. E. T. Fullilove, Shreveport, La.
Vice President................... Mrs. T. K. Faunt Le Roy, New Orleans, La.
Corresponding Secretary............Mrs. C. J. Foster, Shreveport, La.
Recording Secretary................. Miss Lizzie Paxson, Keachie, La.
Treasurer.......................Mrs. S. B. McCutchen, Shreveport, La.
State Organizer ....Mrs. M. C. Alexander, Longstreet, La.

DISTRICT SECRETARIES.

New Orleans District..................Mrs. Linus Parker, New Orleans, La.
Baton Rouge District...
Opelousas District................. ...Mrs. Thos. S. Randle, Lafayette, La.
Alexandria District...........................Mrs. R. Horn, Keachie, La.
Shreveport District..................Mrs. M. H. Morrison, Shreveport, La.
Arcadia District...........................Mrs. Jessie Bond, Ruston, La.
Delhi District..........................Miss Minnie Thompson, Delhi, La.

NEW ORLEANS METHODIST DEPOSITORY.

TRUSTEES.

Rev. J. B. Walker, President; Dr. John W. Adams, Secretary; Wm. B. Thomson, Treasurer; Bishop J. C. Keener, Dr. J. J. Lyons, John H. Campman, Jno. G. Grant, Benj. O, L. Rayne.

LEGAL CONFERENCE.

Rev. C. W. Carter, President; Rev. J. T. Sawyer, Secretary; Revs. C. Keener, T. K. Faunt Le Roy, J. A. Miller, F. N. Parker; and W. B. Thomson, Lyman S. Widney and T. J. Williams.

Resolved, That the Conference Board of Trustees be instructed to hold a meeting at every session of the Conference, and to make a report in due form to the Conference of their proceedings, and all matters in their charge.

Resolved, That the Act of Incorporation be published annually in the printed Minutes.

ACT OF INCORPORATION.

An Act to Incorporate the Louisiana Annual Conference of the Methodist Episcopal Church, South.

Section 1. Be it enacted by the Senate and House of Representatives of the State of Louisiana, in General Assembly convened, That John C. Keener, H. N. McTyeire, J. Saunders, R. Randle, J. B. Walker, S. J. Davies, L. Parker, Philo M. Goodwyn and L. A. Reed, and their associates and successors, such as the Louisiana Conference may from time to time see proper to appoint, be and they are hereby created a body politic and corporate under the name and style of the "Louisiana Conference of the Methodist Episcopal Church, South," and be capable of suing and being sued, entering into contract, receiving and holding property for educational purposes as may from time to time be specified by the said Conference at its annual session, either by donation or purchase.

Sec. 2. Be it further enacted, etc., That the domicile of said corporation shall be located in the City of New Orleans, and the affairs thereof shall be managed by nine trustees, to be appointed by the Louisiana Annual Conference, one of whom shall be elected President. The president and four trustees shall form a quorum, and shall have power to appoint all other officers necessary for conducting its affairs, and make and adopt such rules, by-laws and regulations as they may deem proper for the management of said corporation, provided that the same be in conformity with the laws and regulations of the Methodist Episcopal Church, South, and not repugnant to the laws of the State.

JOHN M. SANDIDGE,
Speaker of the House of Representatives.

Approved March 15, 1855.   ROBT C. WICKLIFFE,
President of the Senate.

P. G. HEBERT,
A true copy: Governor of the State of Louisiana.
ANDREW S. HERRON.

Legal Form of Incorporations for Church Property.

ACT OF INCORPORATION.

STATE OF LOUISIANA, }
  Parish of —— }

We, the undersigned, do hereby form ourselves into a Corporation, to acquire and enjoy the rights, privileges and powers of a body Corporate under the provisions of an Act of the Legislature of Louisiana, approved March 14, 1855, entitled "An Act for the Organization of Corporations for Literary, Scientific, Religious and Charitable purposes.

ARTICLE I.

The title of this Corporation shall be (here insert the title of the Corporation)

ARTICLE II.

The objects of this Corporation are to acquire and hold lands, houses and other property, for the use and enjoyment of the members of the Methodist Episcopal Church, South, and who now hold or may hereafter hold their membership at —— ——; it being especially intended to secure the said Church members a house in which they may worship Almighty God, and the free use of the pulpit to the Ministers and Preachers of the said Methodist Episcopal Church, South, and also to secure a Parsonage for their Minister.

ARTICLE IV.

The members of this Corporation, a majority of whom shall constitute a quorum, shall be a Board of Trustees, and they shall elect from among their number, at their first meeting, a President and a Secretary, who shall also act as Treasurer, who shall hold their offices for one year, and until their successors are chosen. The Board of Trustees may remove these officers, and elect their successors, at any time by a majority vote The property shall be held, and suits brought and defended, in name of the President and Trustees of the (here insert the title of the Corporation) Citation shall be made upon the President at his residence. In the execution of any deed or act of the Board of Trustees, the signature of the President shall be sufficient. Vacancies may occur in the Board and shall be filled in the manner and by the authorities provided for the appointment of Trustees by the Discipline of the Methodist Episcopal Church, South, and this Corporation shall be governed by the laws and usages of the said Methodist Episcopal Church, South, in so far as they are not inconsistent with the laws of this State and the tenor and meaning of these articles of incorporation.

ARTICLE V.

This Corporation shall continue and exist for ninety-nine years.

NOTE.—These articles must be dated and signed in presence of two witnesses, by more than six members of the Methodist Church, and then taken to the District Attorney, who must examine and certify that it is in accordance with the law, and then the Articles must be recorded in the office of the Parish Recorder, after which the Board may meet, elect their officers, transact business, receive titles, etc.

DISTRICT CONFERENCE.

The following is the rule respecting the organization of the District Conference :

The District Conference shall be composed, first, of all the preachers, traveling and local, in the District; and second, of one lay delegate from every sixty members, or fractional part thereof, within the bounds of each circuit, station and mission in the district. The lay members shall be elected by the several Quarterly Conferences, and no Quarterly Conference shall be denied two lay delegates.

MISCELLANEOUS.

RESOLUTIONS.

The following were unanimously adopted :

WOMAN'S WORK.

Resolved, That we hail with pleasure the advent of Mrs. Lyons, Mrs. Russ, and Mrs. Faunt Le Roy among us, and that we have listened with pleasure and profit to their reports and cheering words ;

Resolved, That we heartily endorse the design of the Woman's Home Mission and Parsonage Society and the Woman's Foreign Missionary Society, and pledge ourselves to do all in our power to help these women in the accomplishment of their important work.   THOMAS J. UPTON,
ROBERT H. WYNN.

BISHOP A. G. HAYGOOD.

WHEREAS, The morning dispatches convey the sad intelligence that Bishop A. G. Haygood, one of our Chief Pastors, lies at the point of death at his home near Atlanta, Ga.; therefore be it

Resolved, That we, the Louisiana Annual Conference, now in session, do hereby express our Christian sympathy for his family in this hour of anxiety and sorrow ; and that we pray our Heavenly Father that he may be restored for many years of usefulness   S S. KEENER,
C. W. CARTER.

FIFTIETH SESSION.

WHEREAS, The next session of our Annual Conference will be the fiftieth session since its organization ;

Resolved, That Rev. R. J. Harp be requested to preach a sermon appropriate to the occasion, upon the first day of the next session at 7 p. m.

H. S. JOHNS,
THOS. J. UPTON.

THANKS.

Resolved, That the Conference desires to express its appreciation of the kind and hospitable treatment which it has received at the hands of the Louisiana Avenue Church, and of New Orleans Methodism in general, and to the citizens of New Orleans who have taken part in the entertainment of the Conference ;

That we express our thanks to the Railroad Companies which have granted favors ; and to the Daily Press for their full reports of proceedings.

W. WINANS DRAKE,
H. S. JOHNS,
J. L. PIERCE.

CONFERENCE ROLL FOR 1895.

Name.	Post Office.
P. H. Diffenweirth	Largo, Florida
James L. Wright	Vernon, La
John A. Miller	Ruston, La
B. F. White	Delhi, La
Thos. H. McClendon	Brodnax, La
Jesse Fulton	Coushatta, La
Thomas J. Upton	Lisbon, La
Joseph H. Stone	Ruston, La
John F. Wynn	Baker, La
Henry O. White	Opelousas, La
Charles W. Carter	Jackson, La
E. W. Yancey	Funny Louis, La
Marcus C. Manly	Washington, La
Robt. Parvin	Gibbsland, La
Robt. A. Davis	Oak Ridge, La
Robert Randle	Shiloh, La
Christopher R. Godfrey	Floyd, La
George Jackson	Lecompte, La
Reynolds S. Trippett	Doncaster, England
John M. Brown	Many, La
Enos B. Foust	Rayne, La
Thomas S. Randle	Lafayette, La
Jacob D. Harper	Homer, La
Robert S. Isbell	Calhoun, La
Felix G. Hocutt	West Lake, La
John T. Sawyer	New Orleans, La
Joseph B. Walker	Algiers, La

Name.	CONFERENCE ROLL FOR 1895—continued.	Post Office.
John M. Johnston		Pineville, La
N. S. Cornell		Haughton, La
Lewis A. Reed		New Orleans, La
James A. Parker		Morgan City, La
J. F. Patterson		Montgomery, La
T. K. Faunt Le Roy		New Orleans, La
John B. Cassity		Minden, La
Samuel S. Keener		Baton Rouge, La
John L. P. Sheppard		Mansfield, La
James M. Beard		New Iberia, La
R. M. Blocker		Jeannerette, La
Charles T. Munholland		Lecompte, La
Reuben S. Colier		Haynesville, La
Samuel H. Whatley		Prudhomme, La
Robert J. Harp		Lake Charles, La
F. D. Van Valkenburgh		Pattersonville, La
Thomas B. White		Ruston, La
Stephen J. Davies		Alexandria, La
Daniel C. Barr		Downsville. La
J. B. A. Ahrens		New Orleans, La
H. J. Boltz		Plain Dealing, La
Wilson Moore		Atlanta, La
J. F. Scurlock		Bunkie, La
James Ivy Hoffpaufr		Boyce, La
Franklyn N. Parker		New Orleans, La
J. S. Sanders		Rayne, La
Henry S. Johns		Plaquemine, La
Houston Armstrong		Franklin, La
J. O. Bennett		Zachary, La
Robt. P. Howell		Lake Arthur, La
William H. Hill		Grand Cane, La
Harry W May		Arcadia, La
S. S. Holliday		Pelican, La
A. D. McVoy		Mansfield, La
Fitzgerald Sale Parker		New Orleans, La
Christian Keener		New Orleans, La
William J. Porter		Indian Bayou, La
John B. Williams		Pleasant Hill, La
James E. Riddle		Coushatta, La
C. Marcy Lyons		New Orleans, La
William F. Henderson		Greenwood, La
James E. Densen		Bunkie, La
John F. Foster		Delhi, La
Charles F. Staples		Vernon, La
James J. Kelly		Abbeville, La
W. H. LaPrade		Shreveport, La
J. L. Pierce		New Orleans, La
J. H. Brown		Gannsville, La
Henry H. Ahrens		New Orleans, La
Isaac T. Reames		Girard, La
William G. Evans		West Monroe, La
William Schuble		Rosedale, La
E. L. Singeltary		Amite City, La
J. White Davis		Bienville, La
James M. Henry		New Orleans, La
W. Winans Drake		Crowley, La

Name.	CONFERENCE ROLL FOR—1895 continued.	Post Office.
Herman W. Knickerbocker		Lake Providence, La
Benjamin H. Sheppard		Ringgold, La
H. Milton Banks		Eden, La
Samuel S. Bogan		Slaughter, La
James Russell Roy		Columbia, La
John B. Kent		Bayou Chicot, La
William D. Gaskins		Farmerville, La
M. G. Jenkins		Bastrop, La
Berry T. Crews		Mansfield, La
Albert S. Lutz		Shreveport, La
Robert H. Wynn		New Orleans, La
Lyman F. Jackson		Alexandria, La
Noel B. Norwood		Daisy, La
William T. Currie		Covington, La
R. W. Tucker		Wilson, La
H. R. Singleton		Jackson, La
V. D. Skipper		Homer, La
Geo. D. Anders		Blairstown, La
Paul M. Brown		Keachie, La
Nathan J. Roberts		Greensburg, La
J. P. Haney		Pine Grove, La
P. A. Johnston		Jackson, La
E. N. Evans		Monroe, La

ON TRIAL.

John W. Lee		Spring Creek, La
Harry W. Rickey		Natchitoches, La
Elton Wilson		Pollock, La
Williams E. Akin		Gilbert, La
W. T. Woodward		Simsport, La
George P. White		Pontchatoula, La
W. H. Benton		Franklinton, La
Tatum M. Wafer		Waterproof, La
S. B. Beall		Clinton, La
N. E. Joyner		Vanderbilt University, Nashville, Tenn
R. R. Randle		Prairieville, La
W. B. Van Valkenburgh		Cameron, La
A. W. Turner		Big Cane, La
Talbot A. Luster		Bayou Sara, La
Willie A. Clarke		Talisheek, La
Robert C. Grace		Glenmora, La
Chester R. Seward		Magnolia, La
Ed. T. Densen		Opelousas, La
Albert S. J. Neill		St. Martinsville, La
Robert W. Vaughan*		Homer, La
James Jesse Smylie		Amite City, La
Robert W. Randle		Lake Charles, La
Charles C. Miller		Jackson, La
W. D. Pickens		Vinton, La
Ira Lincoln Bronson		Winsboro, La
Earl Leslie Alford		Harrisonburg, La
Wiley Griffin Roberts		Franklinton, La
Louis E. Wicht		Centenary College, Jackson, La

LAY DELEGATES.

New Orleans District.

Col. David Zable,   C. L. Andrews,
W. B. Thomson,   E. P. Mackie.

ALTERNATES.

T. J. Reames,*   M. C. Aldrich.*

Baton Rouge District.

Hon. H. C. Newsom, A. N. Brown,
Col. I. D. Wall,   L. G. Gowers.

Opelousas District.

Capt. J. N. Pharr,   S. N. Currie,*
U. T. Blacksher,*   C. P. Hampton.*

ALTERNATES.

W. S. Evins,*   J. M. Daniel,*
           A. M. Mayo.

Alexandria District.

H. H. White,   Noel Norwood,*
H. G. Goodwyn,   J. B. Pickles.

ALTERNATES.

Daniel Brewer,*   Robt. McGimsey.*
*Not present.

Shreveport District.

3. B McCutchen,   W. G. Wadley,
Rev. John Franklin, J. W. Taylor.

ALTERNATES.

T. J. Jackson,*   W. R. Jackson.*

Arcadia District.

Dr. R. Roberts,*   Rev. F. M. Henry,*
J. B. Williams,*   R. T. McClendon.*

ALTERNATES.

J. W. Dawson,*   J. T. Baker.

Delhi District.

Dr. A. S. Helmick, Samuel Whited,
E. E. Riggs,*   Rev. A. W. Moore.*

ALTERNATES.

A. D. O. Moore,*   D. T. Chapman.*

REPORTS OF BOARDS AND COMMITTEES.

REPORT OF COMMITTEE ON CHURCH PUBLICATIONS.

The printing press is one of the recognized instruments of power of our time. Every enterprise, secular and religious, recognizes the necessity for this arm of power. All religious organizations appreciate the potency of this written voice to disseminate their views and propagate their peculiar polity and doctrine. If this be an age of reading it is also true that much of the present day literature is of a sensational and vicious character. There is a winged, flying host of this literature. It is as omnipresent as the flies and frogs of Egypt and more loathsome and contaminating. It is the opinion of your Committee that the only way to avert this plague is by the substitution of literature that is pure and wholesome.

It is a matter of felicitation that the literature coming from our House is uniformly of an uplifting and healthful nature.

The Methodist press is doing its part in illuminating and elevating fallen and benighted man.

Your Committee repeats, with emphasis, its belief that we are multiplying papers beyond the limits of sound policy and at the expense of failing to reach the highest efficiency in this field of usefulness. We think that fewer papers, a larger circulation, and better papers should be our motto. Without this our Christian Advocates. can never be the instruments of power they should be. (The Book Committee have felt themselves authorized in appropriating $............ of the produce of the Publishing House to the superanuates and widows and orphans of deceased traveling preachers of the M. E. Church, South.) The Sunday-school Department increases in popularity, usefulness and prosperity. Our Methodist Review is a very able and instructive periodical, and merits a wider reading than it has secured. Our preachers and laymen should become subscribers of this interesting and able publication. We notice with pleasure that it has been changed from a quarterly to a bi-monthly and that the editor in visiting from conference to conference is reaping an ample harvest of subscriptions. Since our last report the *Epworth Era*, the official organ of our young people's movement has made its appearance. We greet kindly its bright face. As its recent unfortunate utterance has been repented of, we hope that forgiveness will be complete, and that henceforth it will spread only the "words of truth and soberness." Our connectional organ, the *Nashville Christian Advocate*, is more than self-sustaining and approximates the ideal both in its mechanical and literary execution. We should generally subscribe for it and heartily sustain it. Our own excellent organ, the *New Orleans Advocate*, gives every indication of having taken a new lease on life and increasing prosperity. Before it can attain its maximum of influence and usefulness, there is much inertness and apathy to be overcome. Let all our preachers make public appeals and private solicitations. in its behalf. Let us not only resolve, but heartily and promptly do, until our united efforts shall lift our paper to the plane it ought to occupy in the public favor. It is edited with ability, filled with useful and interesting matter, neatly printed and issued from a great commercial center.

Resolved, That we approve of the management of our various publishing interests at Nashville and commend the Publishing House to the favor and patronage of our people.

Resolved, That we will do more to aid our editor and publisher in extending among our people the circulation of our *New Orleans Advocate*.

Resolved, That S. S. Keener, J. M. Beard and J. B. A. Ahrens, be continued as the Publishing Committee of this Conference.

J. L. PIERCE,
B. F. WHITE,
R. M. BLOCKER.

REPORT OF COMMITTEE ON DISTRICT CONFERENCE RECORDS.

1—The Opelousas District Record was examined and only one error detected. The minutes of the last session were not approved.

2—The Woodville District Record has no marginal notes. The minutes of both sessions of the first day are not approved, and also the minutes of the last session were not approved.

3—The Arcadia District Record was examined and found to be correct.

4—The New Orleans District Record was found to be without marginal notes, and the minutes of the morning session of the second day were not approved, and also the minutes of the last session were not approved.

5—The Delhi District Record was examined and found correct.

6—The Shreveport District Record is very neatly and systematically kept. There is no record of the approval of the minutes of the last session.

7—The Alexandria District Record was not before us.

N. S. CORNELL,
W. W. DRAKE,
H. H. WHITE.

REPORT OF COMMITTEE ON BIBLE CAUSE.

The history of the Reformation and its subsequent evangelical developments presents to the student of civilization and of the kingdom of Christ a record of the power of the printed Bible, the chief factor in the development of both. Contemporaneous with the Reformation was the development of the printer's art, and first among the products of the press was the Word of God. From that time to this, protestant evangelization has relied upon the work of Bible distribution as next in importance only to the proclamation of the Gospel by a living ministry.

The experience of all missionary enterprises, both foreign and domestic, has ever borne witness to the efficacy of the printed Bible, although it be without note or comment. The Word itself is the vehicle of life and the Holy Spirit has set His seal upon this divine book in every language and among all peoples of the world. The facts known to intelligent Christians are sufficient to commend the cause which this committee represents without argument.

Without further comment we call attention to the abstract of the Seventy-eighth Annual Report of the American Bible Society. From this report we learn that the work of the Society is progressing in all departments; the field of operation is enlarging and the facilities for publication are being multiplied. The Society is not only printing in America, but in the regions beyond, from Constantinople to Japan, editions of the Word of God are being issued in many languages and dialects. Not only are many thousands of Bibles and portions being distributed, but there is a work of translation and revision going on all the time which no other missionary organization or denominational publishing house could possibly accomplish with their present resources. Considered from this point of view the work of the American Bible Society presents a claim upon the Church for support and co-operation which cannot be resisted.

Our own Church is fully committed to this work and has placed the collection for the American Bible Society on the register of its required benevolences. And our last General Conference has emphasized this obligation by incorporating this work in the regular minute business of the Annual Conference, and also making it obligatory upon every preacher in charge to present the claims of the Society in his charge once a year and report the contribution secured to the Annual Conference.

This year only about thirty charges have reported any collections, the total amount raised being $341.00, $307.00 of this amount coming from one district. This indicates that the presentation of the cause has not been general. We desire to commend the official literature of the Society, believing that if this is read it will greatly increase the general interest of preachers and people in the work.

F. N. PARKER,
R. M. BLOCKER,
H. C. NEWSOM.

REPORT OF BOARD OF EDUCATION.

The action of the General Conference of our Church creating a General Board of Education was a recognition and an emphasis of a wide spread, if not a universal, sentiment favoring an earnest, well-planned and well-sustained forward movement in Educational matters. This sentiment, which is in perfect accord with the principles of applied Christianity and with the genius of Methodism needs just now proper direction only, for the enlargement and firmer establishment of our Church Schools. To direct this sentiment, in so far as the Methodists of Louisiana are concerned, is the province and the duty of the body of ministers and laymen who constitute this Annual Conference. To fail to direct it will be to neglect conditions of advantage never before offered to us. Now, as in response to every popular demand, the world is quick to offer a supply, if not of the best quality, at least sufficient in extent and in attractiveness, to satisfy a somewhat undiscerning public ; and unless the Church thoroughly equips, sufficiently endows and largely advertises her own institutions of learning without delay, her opportunity will be lost. If effort shall concentrate upon Centenary and Mansfield Colleges, both of noble record and large usefulness, our demand for higher education, at least, will be fully met.

CENTENARY COLLEGE.

Since the last session of this Conference several important changes have been made in the faculty of Centenary College. Dr. W. L. C. Hunnicutt, after years of faithful and excellent work, resigned the presidency of the college, and Dr. C. W. Carter, an honored member of this Conference, was elected his successor, entering upon his duties at the opening of the present session. Two additional instructors were at the same time added to the family—J. M. Sullivan to the chair of physics, and C. C. Wier to the chair of English. As now constituted, the faculty is adequate and able. We congratulate the Board of Trustees and the Methodist public upon the enlargement of facilities thus secured, and note with pleasure the immediate good results in the large number of new students now in attendance. Of the ninety who have matriculated for the session, forty-five are new students. Of these ninety, eight are young preachers, and eleven are sons of preachers. The increase of students over last year's enrollment is 26, with the Spring term increase still to be added. Twenty-six parishes of our own State are represented in the student body, with members also from Texas, Mississippi, Alabama and Hondur as.

The college is in need of funds, both for improvement of buildings and to meet the salaries of the professors. For the former purpose special donations must be secured, and we urge upon our people the wisdom of immediate response to this call. For the latter purpose the interest now due, and falling due, on endowment notes would largely suffice, could this interest be collected. We urge immediate payment. We may be forced to suffer loss from a faculty from which we can not afford to lose a man, if this matter is longer neglected. The college is entering upon what promises to be the most prosperous period of its career, and we can not afford to arrest its progress by depriving it of means.

MANSFIELD FEMALE COLLEGE.

The report of the president of Mansfield College shows an attendance of fifty-nine students the present session, of whom ten are daughters of preachers in this Conference. The establishment of a free high school at Mansfield has drawn from the college patronage largely, and will continue to do so in the future. To compete with this school on the plane of tuition will be impossible so long as the college remains unendowed ; the competition must be on the issue of better advantages to the student, and these advantages the faculty is supplying, and will continue to furnish. The Departments of Music, Art, Foreign Languages and Ancient Languages are all well officered, and the instruction in the Literary Department is extended and thorough. We cordially recommend this excellent school to our membership throughout the Conference.

PAINE AND LANE INSTITUTES.

The colored education work of our Church is confined, so far as Church action is concerned, to Paine Institute, Augusta, Ga , and Lane Institute, at Jackson Tenn. Each of these excellent schools is presided over by a minister of our own Church, and each deserves the hearty sympathy and support of our people. The sum of two hundred dollars is asked of this Conference during the coming year for this work by the General Board of Education, and we urge its collection in full.

The report of the Treasurer of this Board shows the receipts from collections during the year now closing to be four hundred and eighty-two dollars and twenty cents for education, and eighty-six dollars and ten cents for Paine and Lane Institutes. In accordance with the resolution adopted by our Conference at its last session, the fund for education has been divided between Centenary and Mansfield Colleges, Mansfield receiving $206.60, and Centenary $275.60.

Your Board offers for adoption the following resolutions:

Resolved, That the present Board of Managers be continued for Mansfield Female College and for Pierce and Paine College.

Resolved, That Rev. C. W. Carter be appointed president, and Rev. C. C. Miller professor at Centenary College, and Rev. A. D. McVoy president and financial agent at Mansfield Female College.

Resolved. That we cordially invite Prof. C. C. Wier, as agent for Centenary, and Dr. McVoy, agent for Mansfield, to visit the various charges of this Conference in the interest of these institutions.

Resolved, That we instruct the Joint Board of Finance to apportion among the districts of this Conference the amounts asked for by the General Board of Education for our educational work, and for Paine and Lane Institutes.

WM. H. La PRADE,
President.

REPORT OF COMMITTEE ON TEMPERANCE.

We realize that to consume the valuable time of this Conference in discussing the evils of the traffic in alcoholic liquors is unnecessary.

Surely every thoughtful man among us is fully aware of the fact that one of the most formidable enemies of the Church of God is to be found in the person of King Alcohol.

We are also mindful of the fact that the M. E. C. S. has recognized the opposition of this enemy, and expressed herself repeatedly in no uncertain language—declaring that "the liquor traffic can never be licensed without sin;" and further, that "we are a prohibition church." By our general rules our Church is resolved into a total abstinence society, and none of our members may consistently indulge in social drinking. This advanced position is one of which every Methodist may well be proud, and still the results are so meagre, that we are led to fear that we have not done our whole duty. Our theory is admirable, but our practice is imperfect.

We have all observed that the liquor traffic does not fear resolutions, because as a general thing they are ineffective. And just so long as we continue to pass meaningless resolutions, just so long are we the object of the ridicule of those engaged in the whisky business.

What we need is real effective opposition. And to the accomplishment of that purpose, some well defined policy must be adopted.

Therefore, be it Resolved, That we recommend that our preachers begin by laboring with those members of our several charges who sell or drink intoxicating liquors; and if they refuse to conform to the rules of our church, we will proceed as the discipline directs in such cases.

And be it further Resolved. That we will preach at least one sermon during the coming year on the subject of total abstinence, and one sermon on prohibition.

And be it further Resolved, That we will use every possible effort, both in public and in private, to secure prohibition in the parishes where we reside.

C. M. LYONS,
T. J. UPTON,
R. S. COLIER.

REPORT OF SUNDAY SCHOOL BOARD.

We recognize that the Sunday School is an important factor in church work and that without it our children, or at least a large per cent of them, would never be trained and instructed in scriptural truths.

The School as designed was not intended to take the place of home instruction, but nevertheless, the fact stares us in the face; and, since this is so, we see the absolute importance of Sunday School work and the necessity of devoting much time and thought thereto. It is the nursery where the plant is to be trained and nursed that it may afterward bloom in and adorn the church of God.

We deeply deplore, however, the fact, that the people seem to have the idea that the Sunday School is for the young alone; and we would suggest to, and seek to impress upon, the superintendents the fact that the grown people are needed in the school and should be there as well as the young. By reason of the absence of older people and their seeming indifference to this work, superintendents are often, if not nearly always, compelled to take young and inexperienced parties as their teachers.

We note very few missionary societies in our schools and would call attention to the fact that every school ought to be a missionary society. Our discipline states that there should be held in each district an Annual Sunday School Conference. So far we have heard of but three districts which have so done, viz: Opelousas, Delhi and Shreveport. Those held in Opelousas and Delhi districts were especially interesting.

We hope the brethren will hold these meetings. We would also call attention to the Interdenominational State Sunday School Convention, which is to meet at Lake Charles next year and request that the presiding elders appoint delegates from their several districts, who will go and be in attendance.

This work is a grand thing, brethren, for we should not neglect the lambs and in order not so to do we should get in touch with advance work and methods along this line.

We would again, as last year, call attention to and request that the presiding elders turn in each year a written statement of the amount expended on Sunday Schools in their several districts and where so expended. The Board in studying the discipline, note that they are called upon to hold an Annual Convention of all Sunday School workman and hardly seeing their way clear to so do, have thought best that during the session of our Annual Conference one night be given up to the Sunday School work; we suggest that Friday night be so occupied.

We have had laid before us considerable matter in reference to the Epworth League, and in reviewing it have been impressed with the fact that by these instrumentalities much good may and can be accomplished.

We would stress it upon the brethren that they organize Leagues where practicable and seek to broaden the circulation of the *Epworth Era.*

The following disbursements of amounts have been made for this year as per request from the various presiding elders:

Opelousas District..... .... $114 00
New Orleans District..:........ ....:................ .... 89 00
Alexandria District.......................:.............. .... 50 00
Shreveport District............... .. .. 10 00

JNO. F. FOSTER,

President.

'REPORT OF SECRETARY OF CONFERENCE BOARD OF MISSIONS.

During the past year the Board has helped the following charges: New Orleans District:—Lower Coast Mission, 100.00; Carrollton, $50.00; Grosse Tete and False River, $100.00. Shreveport District:—City Mission, $200 00; Victoria, $62.50; West Natchitoches, $62.50. Arcadia District:—La Pine, $50.00; Sparta, $75 00. Delhi District:—P. E. $50,00; Oakley, $75.00; Floyd, $100.00. Opelousas District:—French Mission, $150.00; Jackson St., and West Lake, $100.00; Sulphur Mine. $50.00. Alexandria District:—P. E. $200 00; Nugent, $50.00; Ada, $50 00; Winfield, $50.00. We have aided sixteen charges and two presiding elder's districts, appropriating $1575.00 to needy sections of the work in our State.

The collections for Foreign Missions during the past year have fallen off slightly while those of Domestic work show a slight increase. In view of the financial condition of the country this year the results are not discouraging.

For the coming year we have appropriated to the Domestic Mission work $1565.00, divided as follows among the several districts:—New Orleans, $270 00; Shreveport, $315.00, Alexandria, $275.00; Opelousas District, $260.00; Arcadia District, $65.00; Delhi District, $120.00; Baton Rouge District, $260.00; being a total of $1565.00. We needed at least $1000.00 more. We wish now to emphasize the necessity of enlarging this fund. If we could secure larger collections for this cause it would be possible to concentrate our work and enable us to accomplish twice as much as is now being done.

We desire to call the attention of the Conference to the recent "Forward Movement" in missions projected by the General Board of Missions. The Board has requested us to take action with regard to the following particulars:

First, by securing the appointment of a Conference Secretary. If financial or other conditions do not admit of his employ for travel, he could, at least, conduct all necessary correspondence in arranging for missionary mass meetings, concerts of prayer, and dissemination of Missionary information.

Second, by requesting the Presiding Elders to act as district secretaries. They would in that capacity co-operate with the Conference Secretaries, and in pursuance of the Disciplinary provisions already noted, aid the preachers in carrying out the plans of the General and Conference Boards.

Third, by recognizing the preacher in charge as the local secretary who would devise plans for securing the missionary collections, foreign and domestic, organize his Sunday Schools into Missionary Societies, and lead the monthly concert of prayer for missions. Such work would be most appropriate, since by the enactment of the General Conference he is made responsible for the holding of missionary meetings, the circulation of missionary literature and the education and inspiration of his people.

We regard this as a very important movement, and, hence, the Conference Board by vote resolved to incorporate the above in the annual report.

In compliance with the above request of the General Board, the Conference Board recommends the appointment of a Conference Secretary who shall attend to the various duties suggested, provided that this does not involve the appoint-

ment of a man to this work alone, as the Conference Board is not able to under-
take the support of a traveling Secretary.

ASSESSMENTS FOR 1895.

		Foreign Missions.	Domestic Missions.
New Orleans District		$2350 00	$ 800 00
Baton Rouge	"	1000 00	400 00
Shreveport	"	1350 00	550 00
Arcadia	"	1350 00	550 00
Opelousas	"	1100 00	450 00
Alexandria	"	600 00	250 00
Delhi	"	1250 00	400 00
Totals		$9000 00	$3400 00

Resolved, That all amounts of $25.00 be paid in full and all others quarterly.

F. N. PARKER,
Secretary.

REPORT OF THE CORRESPONDING SECRETARY OF THE LOUISIANA CONFERENCE WOMAN'S MISSIONARY SOCIETY.

"In a conversation once with a friendly Hindoo on the subject of Christian Missions, Dr. Henry Martyn Clark said to him: 'Do you mind telling me which of all our methods you fear most?' 'Why should I put weapons in the hands of the enemy?' was the reply; 'but I will tell you. We do not greatly fear your schools; we need not send our children. We do not fear your books, for we do not read them. We do not much fear your preaching; we need not listen. But *we dread your women and we dread your doctors*, for your doctors are winning our hearts, and your women are winning our homes, and when our hearts and homes are won, what is left to us?' This winning of hearts and homes is what the Woman's Missionary Society is endeavoring to do; for this the Board plans, prays and seeks to bring into action the reserved force of woman's unused energy." Thus speaks our Foreign Secretary, giving to the church at large, in this brief summary, our *raison d'etre*.

The Home Work of the Woman's Board is represented by Conference Societies, 35; Auxiliary Societies, 3318; members, 72,588. Amount contributed during the year, from March 1, 1893, to March 1, 1894, $66,008.83. Since the organization, including money received for Training School, $889,261.66 has been collected.

Literature.—The Woman's Missionary *Advocate*, the organ for adults, has a circulation of 13,000; the *Little Worker*, organ for juveniles, has a circulation of 9,000. A variety of fine leaflets on missionary topics, also maps of our mission fields have been published, amounting to two million, five hundred and fifteen thousand pages.

Missionaries—Thirty-seven are supported by the Society, and distributed as follows: 16 in China, 13 in Mexico, 8 in Brazil, besides many helpers in the Indian Mission.

Foreign Work.—The Board has work in China, Mexico, Brazil and Indian Mission. Reports represent all the work prospering. There are 12 boarding schools, and 40 day schools in successful operation, with an aggregate of 4000 women and children under instruction.

Bible Woman's Work is increasing in every field, much house to house visiting is done, and many are gladly hearing the word of life.

The work in the Louisiana Conference Society still maintains its hold upon the hearts and consciences of the Christian women of the church, While many societies have dropped out, others have been reorganized, and new ones have come in, and the present year marks a small increase in membership. The Conference Society is represented by 27 Auxiliaries, 618 members, 15 Juvenile Societies, with 326 members, making the total membership 944. This very small proportion of the whole membership of the church, whose members are largely women, will doubtless suggest to all pastors the imperative need of their cordial co-operation in "helping these women," in this supremely important work, which was entrusted *first to Mary*, when her Lord said, "go tell my disciples," on that Easter morning eighteen hundred years ago.

The Woman's Missionary Society again asks of the pastors a personal interest in their cause, that where no organization exists they will form one; where it is weak and discouraged they will up-build it; where the love of many has waxed cold in the cause, they will exhort to better things. "Inasmuch as ye have done it unto the least of these, ye have done it unto me."

MRS. CLAIBORNE J. FOSTER,
Cor. Sec. La. Conf. W. M. S.

ADDRESS OF THE VICE-PRESIDENT OF THE CONFERENCE WOMAN'S MISSIONARY SOCIETY.

In the name of the W. F. M. Society of Louisiana we greet you, and would tell something of the work accomplished by us during the past twelve months. We planned for, hoped and prayed and expected, greater results than we see. It is ours to put forth the effort, to plant the seed. It is God's to water and give the increase. We have not been idle, and while conscious that we have not done all we might have done, we know that the year has not been unfruitful. Our State Organizer, Sister Alexander, has done good service. She has organized new societies where none existed, and re-organized and infused new life into many that were languishing. In every case the preachers have sustained her, and recognized her work as being legitimate, and have bidden her "God speed;" for which, dear brethren, we thank you. It makes our work so much easier, to be thus assured of your co-operation and sympathy. The District Conference held in this city last Spring was an interesting occasion, productive of good. And our annual meeting at Lecompte was, indeed, a feast of good things to all who attended. There have not been as many Juvenile and Young People's Societies organized this year as in other years, from the fact that in most every Sunday School there is a Missionary Society, and in the Church an Epworth League, which supplies work for the children and young people.

We regret that the Woman's Board has now, no Missionary from Louisiana in the foreign fields. Our own Miss Sallie Philips has recently married, thus severing her connection with the Woman's Board. We are praying the Lord of the harvest to raise up from our midst some consecrated woman to take her place.

In the field of Missions there is a work for each and every one. Home and Parsonage work should never be neglected. I speak feelingly on this subject. It is essential that our preachers should have comfortable homes, and not be harassed and worried about providing a shelter for their loved ones. This is a needed work, and lies near to every preacher's heart, and nearer to the heart of every preacher's wife. Home Missions are important and seem our first duty, for the fields are white unto harvest, all around us, even at our doors. In this city there are thousands of poor, neglected souls starving for the bread of life. And in the rural districts of our State can be found communities which are in heathen darkness. They know nothing of Jesus and his love, nothing of the joys of religion. These things ought not so to be. It is our duty to carry unto them the living water.

While Home Missions should receive our attention, Foreign Missions are never to be neglected. We are criminal in every sense if we heed not the commission, "Go ye into all the world and preach the Gospel to overy creature." Can we ourselves hope for salvation if we neglect to obey this command?

Nineteen centuries have passed away, and only one-third of the population of the earth is christianized even nominally. It is said there are eight hundred millions to whom the name of Jesus Christ is unknown, and that in China alone fourteen hundred die every hour without hope in God.

The conversion of the whole world is a work of such magnitude that it could only be conceived in the mind of Deity and be made possible by the incarnation of the Son of God. To the human mind it seems impossible, but to the eye of faith it is attainable, for "all things are possible with God." His promises are "yea and amen." And he hath said to his Son : "I will give thee the heathen for thine inheritance, and the uttermost parts of the earth for thy possession." In this great work of evangelizing the world and bringing souls to Christ, woman has a special work given her to do, and which she alone can accomplish; and which she has undertaken, and with God's help is doing in an humble, quiet way. One hundred years ago Women's Missionary Societies were unknown. To-day there are nearly thirty such societies in America alone, with twenty-five thousand auxiliaries, contributing nearly two million dollars annually. This woman's work for woman has been and will continue to be, an inspiration to our church, which has resulted in carrying the glad tidings to thousands of women in heathen lands.

Oh! that every child of God may feel the burden of immortal souls, and realize that the Father requires faithful, loving service from each of his children.

> "Let none hear you idly saying,
> 'There is nothing I can do'
> While the souls of men are dying,
> And the Master calls for you.
> Take the task he gives you gladly,
> Let his work your pleasure be;
> Answer quickly, when he calleth,
> 'Here am I, send me, send me.' "

MRS. T. K. FAUNT LE ROY,
Vice-Pres. of the W. F. M. S. of the Louisiana Conference.

REPORT OF THE WOMAN'S PARSONAGE AND HOME MISSION SOCIETY OF THE LOUISIANA CONFERENCE.

The Woman's Parsonage and Home Mission Society, of the Louisiana Conference, was organized in New Orleans, Dec. 3, 1891. Previous to that time, however, there were in existence several independent auxiliaries doing some excellent work. As all organizations have their difficulties in the beginning, so this society, being unable to provide the means of sending some one forth, to present the needs of this work to our people throughout the Conference, and to create a deeper interest in the new auxiliaries, made slow progress, or we would by this time have grown into a flourishing society.

Of the 18 original auxiliaries, only 10 existed at our last annual meeting. Three auxiliaries were organized during 1893. At present the Conference Society has 19 adult and 7 juvenile auxiliaries, with a membership of about 362 adults and 173 juveniles. It is very important indeed to enlist the children as they make such enthusiastic and diligent workers when rightly interested.

Mrs. E. E. Wiley, our beloved President, was with us at the annual meeting in February, 1894. Her visit was a blessing to all, giving fresh courage, strength and enthusiasm; and she won all hearts by her devotion to her blessed Redeemer. At the conclusion of the meeting, Mrs. Wiley, and our State Organizer, Miss Mary Werlein, made a trip through a portion of the State and formed auxiliaries. They reported the people ready to respond, after the needs and objects of our work were explained. The employing of a State Organizer is the best way to build up the work; because nothing but active, personal effort will multiply our societies, and develop that strength which we need. Her success will depend upon the assistance rendered by the Pastors, in presenting the work favorably to the women of their charges. The office of District Secretary is a valuable arm of the service and strengthens the hands of the Conference Secretary; her success depends upon the help and co-operation of the Presiding Elder.

Brethren, we ask this help in His name, and for His cause. Will you grant it?

Would that all the brethren give heed to the injunction—"Help those women." Dr. Morton says: "The Woman's Parsonage and Home Mission Society is the right arm of the Board of Church Extension. The women of that organization, are pledged to see that every houseless itinerant preacher shall have a home for his family, while engaged in the pastoral work of the church. The motto of the Board of Church Extension, is 'a church for every congregation' and of the Woman's Parsonage Society, 'a home for every preacher.'"

Aid has been given, by our Conference Society, this year, to 4 parsonages: West Lake, Gilbert. Dry Creek, and Abbeville, donating to each, $50.00. There are so many demands upon our society, and the work to be done is so great, that the necessity of multiplying organizations is realized as the only permanent way of increasing our receipts.

The amount received by the Conference Treasurer this year is $472.14. This sum does not include the local work done by the auxiliaries. It is said that missionary societies ought to have two wings—while sending the Gospel to the heathen in foreign lands, we should seek and save the heathen at home. Many of the auxiliaries are doing excellent work along this line, and there is an increasing interest everywhere; still it needs most earnest efforts, for the work will grow in proportion to our energy.

Oh, that God's Spirit may be poured out upon our society, and that many more earnest and consecrated women may join in this work.

In New Orleans we have organized an Industrial School. It is in charge of our City Missionary, Miss Susie Burbank, an earnest, zealous, Christian woman; but the school needs workers, self-sacrificing women of God, to move among the poor, needy and neglected women and children. We have in our city, a Training Class of Christian Workers, who meet weekly, and receive instruction from the City Pastors, and also from Christian physicians on methods and means to be used in Home Mission work.

Humanly speaking success in anything depends upon the individual. Let us so labor that God shall see none more faithful.

We desire a constant interest in your prayers for our Master's guidance and blessing upon our work and labor of love.

We will do our best; results are with the Lord.

MRS. FLORENCE E. RUSS,
Conf. Cor. Secretary.

REPORT OF BOARD OF COLPORTAGE.

We find that our late General Colporteur, F. D. Van Valkenburgh, has succeeded in circulating a large number of our own publications through this and the adjoining Conferences during the last six years. At one time there seemed good reason for believing that a permanent and paying business could be built up in New Orleans.

The employment of a General Colporteur and the opening up of a depot of supplies at Jackson, Miss., by the Mississippi Annual Conference several years ago, seriously interferred with the volume of business done by our General Colporteur at New Orleans. This necessitated the enlarging of the stationery department, and increasing the stocks of general and miscellaneous literature, so as to meet the demands of the local city patronage, and raise the total business to such a condition as to cover costs and expenses of carrying it on.

During the financial stringency of the present year, our Colporteur fell behind with the rent on the store, (No. 9 Chartres street.) occupied by him. The owner of the building quite hastily seized the stock and proceeded against him for the full amount of rent to the expiration of the lease. This action upon her part, so complicated matters as to force the business to the wall.

So far as your Board can determine, our Colporteur did the best he possibly could under these peculiarly trying circumstances, and his integrity, and moral character have been unimpeached and above reproach, for which we are profoundly thankful to the God of all grace.

In view of the financial condition of our territory, your Board has no recommendation to make, farther than to urge that all of our preachers, both traveling and local, will use diligence in endeavoring to place our books in the hands of all our people.

The territory in which we labor is specially needy in this direction. The fact ot the demand for our books being poor, but emphasizes that need the more and appeals to us, as those interested in the enlightenment and salvation of the people, to give our best endeavors to the furtherance of this great work.

J. B. CASSITY, *President.*
F. D VAN VALKENBURGH, *Secretary.*

REPORT OF COMMITTEE ON MEMOIRS.

REV. ALBERT M. WAILES.

The Committee on Memoirs finds itself unable at this time to furnish to the Conference any reliable data of our deceased brother's life and labors amongst us. For many years, Bro. Wailes had been in feeble health, unable to enter upon the pastoral work, and has consequently sustained a supernumerary relation to the Conference, serving God and helping humanity by teaching. Faithful in the execution of this trust, and consistent and pure as a Christian minister, he annually passed the examination of character with the welcome endorsement of his brethren, and their just verdict—"Nothing against him." In the hope and Christian confidence of his brethren, we may surely trust, that the same glad verdict met him at the threshold of our "Father's House."

Your Committee offers the following Resolutions :

Resolved, First, That the prayers and sympathies of the Conference be offered for his bereaved family, and a page of our Minutes devoted to his memory;

Resolved, Second, That the Committee be permitted to prepare a suitable memoir and forward the same to the Secretary of the Conference for publication.

JAMES A. PARKER,
Committee.

NEW ORLEANS DISTRICT.

NAME OF CHARGE.	No. of Local Preachers.	No. of White Members.	No. of Colored Members.	Total Members this year.	Total Members last year.	Additions on Prof. of Faith.	Additions by Certificate and otherwise.	Removals by Death, Cert. and otherwise.	No. of Infants Baptized.	No. of Adults Baptized.	No. t.f Societies in the Charge.	No. of Churches.	Value of Churches.	No. of Parsonages.	Value of Parsonages.	Value of District Parsonage if any.	Value of other Church Property.	Money Expended on Churches and Parsonages.
ndelet St., New Orleans.	3	514	3	520	575	15	67	127	30	3	1	1	35,000 ..	1	15,000	....	100,000 ..	1,526 ..
city Street, " "	1	491	1	493	481	12	26	26	23	2	1	1	31,500 ..					1,500 ..
ne Memorial, " "	1	260	....	261	270	13	32	54	10	3	1	1	30,000 ..					....
isiana Ave., " "	1	306	....	307	316	17	13	39	17	1	1	2	30,000 ..					910 96
eau Street, " "	....	138	....	138	139	2	....	3	8	1	1	1	15,000 ..				250 ..	242 25
colton Ave., " "	....	52	....	52	40	6	7	1	4	....	1	1	5,000 ..					716 52
tna & Craps St. " "	....	158	....	158	143	14	8	7	8	....	2	2	7,500 ..	1	500			180 ..
ker Chapel, " "	....	145	....	145	118	18	13	4	14	5	1	1	6.500 ..					94 05
ades Street, " "	1	148	....	149	120	15	20	6	9	4	1	1	20,000 ..	1	2,000		500 ..	....
uemine & Donaldsonville.	1	112	1	114	103	10	4	3	20	1	2	2	5,000 ..	1	3,000			40 ..
ers	....	132	....	132	124	2	7	1	10	2	1	1	5.000 ..					318 89
on Rouge	....	355	....	355	317	23	30	15	32	7	1	3	26,500 ..	1	2,000		200 ..	200 ..
ss Tete and False River...	....	59	....	59	96	11	2	50	6	1	2	3	3,000 ..					7 ...
er Coast Mission	....	122	1	123	113	10	....	....	4	....	1	1	1,350 ..	1	400			....
Total	8	2992	6	3006	2955	168	219	336	195	30	17	21	$221,350 ..	6	$22,900	..	$102,450 ..	$4,235 67

BATON ROUGE DISTRICT.

NAME OF CHARGE.	No. of Local Preachers.	No. of White Members.	No. of Colored Members.	Total Members this year.	Total Members last year.	Additions on Prof. of Faith.	Additions by Certificate and otherwise.	Removals by Death, Cert. and otherwise.	No. of Infants Baptized.	No. of Adults Baptized.	No. t.f Societies in the Charge.	No. of Churches.	Value of Churches.	No. of Parsonages.	Value of Parsonages.	Value of District Parsonage if any.	Value of other Church Property.	Money Expended on Churches and Parsonages.
son	14	173	....	187	181	6	8	8	2	2	1	1	6,000 ..	1	2,500	..	80,000 ..	64 10
hary	....	119	....	119	98	22	2	3	8	2	1	1	2,500 ..	1	1,112	..	310 ..	200 ..
ou Sara	2	390	....	392	248	28	17	1	15	8	7	6	4,000 ..	1	500			50 ..
son	1	267	....	263	335	25	11	3	10	17	1	4	2,600 ..				175 ..	100 ..
aklinton	2	589	....	591	543	26	25	3	24	21	8	6	2,400 ..	1	800			120 ..
ington	....	214	....	214	198	15	24	23	12	3	6	4	2,500 ..	1	700		300 ..	55 ..
chatoula	3	216	....	219	167	58	2	8	8	34	4	4	2,500 ..	1	400		180 ..	610 ..
e Oak	1	582	....	583	562	30	2	11	24	11	5	5	3,050 ..	1	300		50 ..	1,000 ..
sheek	1	290	....	291	274	21	....	4	31	3	2	2	1,050 ..	1	700		1,450 ..	150 ..
Feliciana	....	726	....	726	662	73	....	9	10	35	4	4	3,500 ..	1	550		500 ..	200 ..
Helena	2	809	....	811	799	5	8	1	20	8	7	7	6,100 ..	1	750			95 ..
t Vincent	1	215	1	217	222	24	6	35	10	9	4	4	1,700 ..				300 ..	130 ..
ite City	2	410	....	412	314	55	52	9	5	23	6	2	2,500 ..	1	800		125 ..	200 ..
iton	....	147	....	147	156	1	1	11	....	1	1	1	1,200 ..	1	600			214 50
aton Rouge	3	589	....	592	576	44	1	29	51	19	10	9	1,800 ..	1	500			400 ..
Total	32	5736	1	5769	5355	483	159	158	230	19	67	60	$43,400 ..	13	$10,212	..	$83,390 ..	$3,588 60

OPELOUSAS DISTRICT.

NAME OF CHARGE.	No. of Local Preachers.	No. of White Members.	No. of Colored Members.	Total Members this year.	Total Members last year.	Additions on Prof. of Faith.	Additions by Certificate and otherwise.	Removals by Death, Cert. and otherwise.	No. of Infants Baptized.	No. of Adults Baptized.	No. t.f Societies in the Charge.	No. of Churches.	Value of Churches.	No. of Parsonages.	Value of Parsonages.	Value of District Parsonage if any.	Value of other Church Property.	Money Expended on Churches and Parsonages.
lousas	....	215	....	215	201	17	8	11	12	4	2	1	2.500 ..	1	2,500	....		275 ..
hington	....	120	....	120	119	8	....	7	2	5	3	2	3,800 ..				175 ..	
uemine Brulé	1	475	....	476	415	68	11	18	23	17	6	3	4,000 ..	1	700		600 ..	190 ..
ayette and Rayne	3	209	....	212	163	45	12	8	5	7	2	2	3,000 ..	1	500			233 50
wley	....	171	....	171	144	27	16	16	10	4	1	1	3,600 ..				70 ..	
eville	....	250	....	250	220	5	30	5	12	3	2	4	4,000 ..	1	600		600 ..	
y Iberia	1	228	....	229	229	7	13	20	7	13	1	1	10,000 ..				367 ..	
iklin	....	140	....	140	122	15	7	5	14	1	1	1	2,500 ..	1	3,500			25 ..
erette	....	70	1	71	61	8	2	....	5	2	1	1	2,000 ..	1	1,500		180 ..	100 ..
Charles	....	215	....	215	233	3	19	40	11	1	1	2	5,500 ..	1	2,250		....	70 75
sou St. and W. Lake	2	84	....	86	64	12	11	1	10	4	1	2	4,500 ..	1	500		41 ..	818 14
ersonville	..	82	....	82	74	4	4	4	9	1	1	1	3.500 ..	1	1,500			750 ..
gan City	1	131	....	132	124	8	....	....	15	6	1	1	3,500 ..	1	700			
hur Mine	....	78	....	78	81	15	2	20	9	4	3	2	500 ..				2 50	
id Cheniere	2	156	....	158	158	11	....	11	24	3	5	1	500 ..				121 60	107 ..
an Bayou	....	459	....	459	366	73	55	35	64	2	3	1	1,570 ..	1	700		100 .:	225 ..
e Arthur	....	126	....	126	106	11	17	8	3	2	1	1	1,200 ..				25 ..	76 35
emout	....																	
lartinsville	....	6	....	6				6		9		1						
Total	10	3215	1	3226	2880	337	213	20	234	79	36	24	$55,670 ..	11	$14,950		$1,245 10	$3,907 74

ALEXANDRIA DISTRICT.

NAME OF CHARGE.	No. of Local Preachers.	No. of White Members.	No. of Colored Members.	Total Members this year.	Total Members last year.	Additions on Prof. of Faith.	Additions by Certificate and otherwise.	Removals by Death, Cert. and otherwise.	No. of Infants Baptized.	No. of Adults Baptized.	No. t.f Societies in the Charge.	No. of Churches.	Value of Churches.	No. of Parsonages.	Value of Parsonages.	Value of District Parsonage if any.	Value of other Church Property.	Money Expended on Churches and Parsonages.
andria	....	121	....	121	109	9	13	10	5	4	1	1	4,000 ..	2	3,500			585 ..
green	....	78	....	78	86	....	13	21	1	....	2	2	4,000 ..					
mpte & White Chapel	2	157	....	159	142	10	11	4	3	2	2	2	3,000 ..					557 25
nsport	....	96	....	96	46	48	4	2	14	15	2	2	1,200 ..	1	250		10 ..	91 45
ille and Big Cane	....	116	....	116	88	26	4	2	12	14	2	2	2,500 ..	1	250		250 ..	600 ..
ng Creek	3	357	....	360	343	30	22	35	22	11	4	4	2,200 ..	1	200		250 ..	340 ..
Creek	....	235	....	235	232	3	5	5	1	1	5	1	100 ..	1	350			50 ..
tgomery	1	311	....	312	287	30	6	11	9	14	2	2	1,150 ..	2	800			66 20
....	1	328	....	329	296	33	10	10	15	12	3	3	400 ..	1	150		50 ..	50 ..
reville	3	372	....	375	326	50	....	1	22	14	4	4	2,000 ..					
mbia	3	190	....	193	190	7	....	4	7	1	2	2	250 ..	1	500			
e and Colfax	....	286	....	286	269	20	7	10	7	3	3	3	4,500 ..	1	700		2,500 ..	10 ..
ville	2	480	....	482	472	45	20	55	52	8	6	4	1,800 ..	1	450		100 ..	25 ..
u Chicot	....	216	....	216	198	32	11	25	29	17	2	2	800 ..	1	300		25 ..	25 ..
nt Mission	1	30	....	31	5	4	25	3	2	2	3	2	1,200 ..				35 ..	332 05
ield	....																	
Total	16	3373		3389	3089	347	151	198	201	118	43	36	$29,100 ..	13	$7,450		$3,195 ..	$2,681 95

ISTRICT.

NAME OF CHARGE.	No. of Pastoral Charges.	No. of Local Preachers.	No. of White Members.	No. of Colored Members.	Total Members this year.	Total Members last year.	Additions on Prof. of Faith.	Additions by Certificate and otherwise.	Removals by Death, Cert. and otherwise.	No. of Infants Baptized.	No. of Adults Baptized.	No. of Societies in the Charge.	No. of Churches.	Value of Churches.	No. of Parsonages.	Value of Parsonages.	Value of District Parsonage if any.	Value of other Church Property.	Money Expended
reveport & City Mission.			475		475	460	30	15	30	11	11	2	2	42,000					
ooringsport.			199		199	199		3	3	3		5	5	300					
ddo		1	233		234	242	2	1	11	3		5	6	5,600	1	1,100			
ansfield			165		165	141	24	12	12	1	12	2	2	3,000	1	2,000			2
any			248		248	232	25	6	12	11	15	4	3	1,600					
bine			280		280	264	15	11	10	8	4	3	3	1,000					
aind Cane			160		160	148	12	5	5	6	10	5	3	2,900	1	400		100	
lacoo and S. Vernon.		3	164		167	167						9	3	1,000	1	150			
ine River			79		79	67		12				4	2	900					
easant Hill			378		378	396	8	4	30	15	8	3	3	3,700	1	600		2,100	
itchitoches			37		37	43		5	11	1		1	1	3,000					
oushatta			130		130	130	1	3	4		1	3	3	2 950	1	500		25	
esley		1	321		322	339	39	8	64	37	10	5	4	2,000	1	350		150	
ed River			28		28	24	4	2	2	1	3	2	2	1,500	1	750			
outh Bossier			242		242	220	28		6	4	20	4	3	3,500	1	500			
orth "			322		32	279	53	21	31	34	25	6	6	3,150 50	2	600		35	
eSoto			362		362	340	24	11	13	5	13	4	4	1,900	1	500			
ort Jessup		2	271		273	264	10		1	10	5	5	4	1,800					
. Natchitoches & Victoria		4	196		200	182	14	4		1	10	9	4	1,000					
Total		11	4290		4301	4137	289	123	248	151	147	81	63	$82.800 50	12	$7,450		$2,410	$4

ARCADIA DISTRICT.

omer		1	205		206	178	41	4	17	8	28	1	1	2,800	1	1,000			
aynesville			348		348	325	23	3	3	1	18	6	4	4,000	1	400			
inden		1	250		251	237	35	4	25		11	3	3	4,000	1	1,000			
inggold		2	365		367	326	37	18	14	30	24	4	4	1,400	1	100			
parta		1	391		392	267	70	80	25	17	60	6	4	1,000					
rcadia		4	493		497	427	70	10	10	8	40	4	3	4,000	1	1,500			
ummerfield		1	568		569	544	16	23	14	4	11	5	4	2,400	1	400			
uston		2	368		370	292	85	28	35	18	42	2	2	3,800	1	1,000		200	
ienna			225		225	210	15				15	2	2	300	1	200			
ernon			324		324	296	60	16	48	11	16	3	3	1,500	1	600		10	
ownsville		1	484		485	471	27	2	15	3	17	5	5	3,000	1	600			
armerville			289		289	277	16	5	9	5	11	3	3	1,500	1	1,300		100	
ulip			331		331	291	54	4	18	10	26	3	3	2,000				100	
alley			378		378	345	30	5	2	6	20	6	3	2,500	1	150			
isbon		1	428		429	405	15	21	12	23	10	5	4	3,700	1	550		230	
alhoun and La Pine.		5	473		478	413	39	34	8	26	38	1	5	3,000	1	450			
annsville		1	184		185	170	13	5	3		3	6	6	1,500	1	200			
Total		20	6104		6124	5474	646	262	258	170	390	65	59	$42.400	15	$9,450		$640 00	$2

DELHI DISTRICT.

ouroe		2	338		340	321	38	12	31	10	10	1	1	3,000	1	2,000			
est Monroe			143	1	144	139		17	12	9	1	3	3	3,800	1	700		225	
astrop		1	123		124	119	2	8	5	6	1	1	1	8,000	1	1,500			
ind Grove		1	267		268	274	9	2	17	5	6	4	4	2,150	1	500		25	
elhi			92		92	74	15	8	5		5	1	1	900	1	500			
loyd		1	276		277	26	14				8	3	3	2,770	1	500			
ake Providence			83		83	86		2	5	2		2	2	2,300	1	800		50	
alr Ridge			172		172	154	12	14	8	15	5	3	3	2,500	1	1,000			
arrisonburg			129		129	120	11		2	8	4	2	2	2,000				75	
aterproof			89		89	85	6	5	7	3		2	2	1,800	1	600		10	
innsboro		1	196		197	185	14	2	4	17	4	3	2	2,350					
ayville			226		226	203	24	1	2	12	16	2	2	1,800	1	500		200	
akley and Vidalia		1	146		147	135	9	17	14	23	2	6	6	3,500	1	325			
Total		7	2280	1	2288	2158	154	88	112	110	62	36	33	$36.9 0	11	$8,925		$585	$2

RECAPITULATION.

ew Orleans District	14	8	2992	6	3006	2955	168	219	336	195	30	17	21	221,350 00	6	22,900		52,450 00	4
hreveport "	19	11	4290		4301	4137	289	123	248	151	147	81	63	82.800 00	12	7,450		2,410 00	4
opelousas "	19	10	3215	1	3226	2880	337	213	209	234	79	36	24	55,670 00	11	14,950		1.245 10	3
lexandria "	16	16	3373		3389	3089	347	151	198	201	118	43	36	29,100 00	13	7,450	2000	3,195 00	2
rcadia "	17	20	6104		6124	5474	646	262	258	170	390	65	59	42.400 00	15	9,450		640 00	2
elhi "	13	7	2280	1	2288	2158	154	88	112	110	62	36	33	36,920 00	11	8,925		585 00	2
aton Rouge "	15	32	5736	1	5769	5335	433	159	158	230	196	67	60	43,400 00	13	10,212	1000	83,390 00	3
Total	113	104	27990	9	28103	26018	2374	1215	1519	1291	1022	345	296	$511,640 00	81	$81,337	5000	$143,915 00	$22
Total last year	96	86	21114	8	21208	19763	1666	871	1632	969	615		241	$468,834 00	62	$64,155	400	$147,127 00	$2
Increase	17	18	*6876	1	*6895	6265	708	344		322	407		55	$42,806 00	19	$17,182	1000		$2
Decrease									113									$3,212 00	$

* This very large increase in membership arises from the addition of a part of the Woodville Dist., Mississippi Con
aving a membership the previous year of 5335. The actual net increase in membership for the year is 2070. † No report last

NAME OF CHARGE.	Presiding Elder.		Preacher in Charge.		Bishops.		Conference Claimants.		For. Miss	
	Ass'd.	Paid.	Ass'd.	Paid.	Ass'd.	Paid.	Ass'd.	Paid.	Ass'd.	I
Shreveport—First Church and City Mission..........................	270 ..	270 .	1800 ..	2000 ..	36 ..	36 ..	150 ..	150 ..	240 ..	2
Mooringsport.......................	95 ..	77 55	555 ..	476 45	12 ..	8 ..	55 ..	27 85	85 ..	
Caddo...............................	120 ..	83 85	750 ..	515 05	15 ..	7 50	66 ..	31 40	100 ..	
Mansfield...........................	120 ..	100 35	800 ..	669 27	15 ..	15 ..	65 ..	65 ..	107 ..	
Many...............................	45 ..	23 55	265 ..	200 ..	6 ..	.. ..	24 ..	4 ..	40 ..	
Sabine.............................	28 ..	17 75	300 ..	70 ..	.. ..	.. ..	.. ..	.. ..	18 ..	
Grand Cane.........................	75 ..	52 78	500 ..	351 32	9 ..	9 ..	45 ..	12 15	67 ..	
Anacoco and S. Vernon..............	24 ..	6 85	150 ..	17 75	3 ..	.. ..	7 ..	.. ..	20 ..	
Cane River	35 ..	10 55	250 ..	137 60	5 ..	.. ..	18 ..	.. ..	25 ..	
Pleasant Hill.......................	105 ..	54 95	700 ..	447 86	14 ..	3 ..	56 ..	7 50	95 ..	
Natchitoches........................	90 ..	21 70	600 ..	224 75	10 ..	.. ..	25 ..	.. ..	70 ..	
Coushatta...........................	90 ..	50 35	700 ..	356 80	10 ..	5 ..	50 ..	18 ..	80 ..	
Wesley..............................	60 ..	24 50	500 ..	195 35	8 ..	8 ..	35 ..	14 ..	60 ..	
Red River	52 ..	52 ..	350 ..	382 50	7 ..	.. ..	30 ..	12 75	47 ..	
S. Bossier..........................	70 ..	65 32	600 ..	500 28	12 ..	8 ..	55 ..	27 ..	80 ..	
N. "	82 50	65 60	550 ..	438 97	10 ..	5 ..	44 ...	20 ..	74 ..	
DeSoto..............................	60 ..	40 ..	400 ..	327 50	8 40	2 ..	36 ..	5 ...	54 ..	
Fort Jessup.........................	60 ..	30 ..	400 ..	196 85	6 ..	.. ..	30 ..	.. ..	45 ..	
Victoria and W. Natchitoches........	30 ..	8 ..	275 ..	50 ..	2 ..	.. ..	10 ..	.. ..	20 ..	
Total...............................	1511 50	1055 65	10445 ..	7558 30	188 40	106 50	801 .	394 65	1327 ..	6

ARCADI

Homer..............................	90 00	85 00	700 00	680 45	10 00	10 00	50 00	50 00	90 00	
Haynesville........................	97 00	74 00	600 00	450 00	10 00	8 00	50 00	40 00	91 00	
Minden.............................	97 00	70 00	800 00	671 00	10 00	10 00	50 00	50 00	95 00	
Ringgold...........................	75 00	51 40	485 00	328 15	8 00	5 50	25 00	8 50	65 00	
Sparta	70 00	35 00	600 00	285 00	8 00	2 50	20 00	5 00	70 00	
Arcadia.............................	125 00	108 00	800 00	700 00	15 00	10 00	76 00	40 00	110 00	
Summerfield........................	98 00	74 00	600 00	443 00	10 00	7 50	50 00	37 50	92 00	
Ruston.............................	125 00	97 03	900 00	746 93	15 00	10 00	75 00	72 65	110 00	
Vienna..............................	60 00	36 00	350 00	175 00	9 00	.. ..	46 00	5 00	76 00	
Vernon.............................	70 00	39 50	600 00	341 50	8 00	6 00	30 00	22 00	70 00	
Downsville.........................	100 00	60 00	600 00	444 00	10 00	5 00	35 00	10 00	90 00	
Farmerville........................	75 00	40 50	450 00	308 00	10 00	5 00	50 00	10 00	75 00	
Calhoun and La Pine................	61 00	38 20	600 00	354 55	7 00	5 00	37 00	11 00	46 00	
Tulip...............................	75 00	54 00	525 00	409 55	10 00	7 50	35 00	33 00	85 00	
Valley..............................	65 00	55 75	400 00	345 00	5 00	5 00	25 00	21 85	65 00	
Lisbon..............................	97 00	82 85	700 00	600 00	10 00	10 00	50 00	47 00	95 00	
Gannsville..........................	30 00	30 00	275 00	202 00	8 00	.. ..	40 00	3 00	63 00	
Total...............................	1410 00	1031 23	9985 00	7484 13	163 00	107 00	738 00	466 50	1388 00	6

DELHI·

Monroe.............................	160 ..	160 ..	1000 ..	1000 ..	20 ..	20 ..	75 ..	75 ..	160 ..	10
W. Monroe.........................	80 ..	60 35	400 ..	384 85	12 50	1 75	55 ..	21 75	80 ..	5
Bastrop............................	100 ..	50 ..	600 ..	522 28	10 ..	3 ..	45 ..	20 ..	100 ..	0
Lind Grove.........................	75 ..	.. ..	475 ..	.. ..	10 50	2 ..	35 ..	7 ..	90 ..	0
Delhi...............................	110 ..	90 ..	800 ..	643 55	12 ..	9 ..	65 ..	56 ..	110 ..	15
Floyd...............................	80 ..	51 60	600 ..	223 29	12 50	2 50	45 ..	8 ..	80 ..	..0
Lake Providence....................	110 ..	95 ..	800 ..	546 31	12 50	4 50	65 ..	58 35	110 ..	:8
Oak Ridge..........................	110 ..	84 20	800 ..	619 85	14 ..	5 ..	65 ..	28 05	110 ..	10
Harrisonburg.......................	80 ..	42 ..	560 ..	300 ..	10 ..	5 ..	45 ..	10 ..	45 ..	0
Waterproof.........................	100 ..	46 03	800 ..	370 17	10 ..	5 ..	50 ..	26 85	95 ..	10
Rayville............................	110 ..	105 ..	600 ..	585 26	12 50	8 ..	57 50	40 ..	110 ..	10
Oakley and Vidalia.................	35 ..	15 ..	525 ..	223 75	5 ..	1 ..	30 ..	7 ..	35 ..	0
Winnsboro..........................	95 ..	63 ..	550 ..	380 ..	12 50	5 ..	45 ..	20 ..	95 ..	0
Total...............................	1245 ..	862 18	8510 ..	5799 31	154 ..	71 75	677 50	378 ..	1220 ..	430

RECAPI

New Orleans District................	1670 70	1676 35	12328 00	11137 96	275 00	256 03	1205 00	1011 98	2350 00	15
Shreveport "	1511 50	1055 65	10445 00	7558 30	188 40	106 50	801 00	394 65	1327 00	6
Opelousas "	1261 90	924 25	9163 00	7562 60	159 42	106 05	637 35	443 90	1068 45	6
Alexandria "	663 50	514 35	6675 00	4960 80	93 85	54 05	407 12	172 75	570 00	2
Arcadia "	1410 00	1031 23	9985 00	7484 13	163 00	107 00	738 00	466 50	1388 00	6
Delhi "	1245 00	862 18	8510 00	5799 31	154 00	71 75	677 50	378 00	1220 00	4
Baton Rouge "	1040 00	851 25	9130 00	7557 25	116 00	110 00	431 00	417 50	890 00	4
Total..............................	8802 60	6915 26	66236 00	52060 35	1149 67	811 38	4896 97	3285 28	8813 45	46
Total last year.......	7158 00	5706 89	57344 05	45437 22	1024 40	746 10	4361 91	2927 65	7545 00	44
Increase.......	1644 60	1208 37	8891 95	6623 13	125 27	65 28	535 06	357 63	1268 45	1
Decrease......	......	......	......	......	......	......	......	......	......	

* This amount includes funds for relief of poor, which not being reported separately this year cannot b

9

NAME OF CHARGE.	No. of Pastoral Charges.	No. of Local Preachers.	No. of White Members.	No. of Colored Members.	Total Members this year.	Total Members last year.	Additions on Prof. of Faith.	Additions by Certificate and otherwise.	Removals by Death, Cert. and otherwise.	No. of Infants Baptized.	No. of Adults Baptized.	No. of Societies in the Charge.	No. of Churches.	Value of Churches.	No. of Parsonages.	Value of Parsonages.	Value of District Parsonage if any.	Value of other Church Property.	Money Expended on Churches.
Shreveport & City Mission.			475	....	475	460	30	15	30	11	11	2	2	42,000	..				7
Mooringsport.			199	....	199	199	....	3	3	3	....	5	5	300	..				
Caddo		1	233	....	234	242	2	1	11	3	....	5	6	5,600	..	1	1,100		
Mansfield			165	....	165	141	24	12	12	1	12	2	2	3,000	..	1	2,000		2,t
Many			248	....	248	232	25	6	15	11	15	4	3	1,600	..				
Sabine			280	....	280	264	15	11	10	8	4	3	3	1,000	..				
Grand Cane			160	....	160	148	12	5	5	6	10	5	3	2,900	..	1	400		100 ..
Anacoco and S. Vernon.		3	164	....	167	167	....					9	3	1,000	..	1	150		
Cane River			79	....	79	67	....	12				4	2	900	..				
Pleasant Hill			378	....	378	396	8	4	30	15	8	3	3	3,700	..	1	600		2,100 ..
Natchitoches			37	....	37	48	....	5	11	1	..	1	1	3,000	..				
Coushatta.			130	....	130	130	1	3	4	....	1	3	3	2,950	..	1	500		25 ..
Wesley		1	321	....	322	339	39	8	64	37	10	5	4	2,000	..	1	350		150 ..
Red River			28	....	28	24	4	2	2	1	3	2	2	1,500	..	1	750		
South Bossier			242	....	242	220	28	....	6	4	20	4	3	3,500	..	1	500		
North "			322	....	32	279	53	21	31	34	25	6	6	3,150	50	2	600		35 ..
DeSoto.			362	..	362	340	24	11	13	5	13	4	4	1,900	..	1	500		
Fort Jessup		2	271	....	273	264	10	....	1	10	5	5	4	1,800	..				
W. Natchitoches & Victoria		4	196	....	200	182	14	4	....	1	10	9	4	1,000	..				
Total	11		4290		4301	4137	289	123	248	151	147	81	63	$82.800	50	12	$7,450		$2,410 ..	$4.4

ARCADIA DISTRICT.

Homer		1	205	....	206	178	41	4	17	8	28	1	1	2,800	..	1	1,000		1
Haynesville		....	348	....	348	325	23	3	3	1	18	6	4	4,000	..	1	400		
Minden		1	250	....	251	237	35	4	25	....	11	3	3	4,000	..	1	1,000		
Ringgold		2	365	....	367	326	37	18	14	30	24	4	4	1,400	..	1	100		1
Sparta		1	391	....	392	267	70	80	25	17	60	6	4	1,000	..				
Arcadia		4	493	....	497	427	70	10	10	8	40	4	3	4,000	..	1	1,500		
Summerfield		1	568	....	569	544	16	23	14	4	11	5	4	2,400	..	1	400		8
Ruston		2	368	....	370	292	85	28	35	18	42	2	2	3,800	..	1	1,000		200 ..
Vienna			225	....	225	210	15	....			15	2	2	300	..	1	200		
Vernon			324	....	324	296	60	16	48	11	16	3	3	1,500	..	1	600		10 ..
Downsville		1	484	....	485	471	27	2	15	3	17	5	5	3,000	..	1	600		
Farmerville			289	....	289	277	16	5	9	5	11	3	3	1,500	..	1	1,300		100 ..
Tulip			331	....	331	291	54	4	18	10	26	3	3	2,000	..				100 ..
Valley			378	....	378	345	30	5	2	6	20	6	3	2,500	..	1	150		
Lisbon		1	428	....	429	405	15	21	12	23	10	5	4	3,700	..	1	550		230 ..
Calhoun and La Pine.		5	473	....	478	413	39	34	8	26	38	1	5	3,000	..	1	450		
Gannsville		1	184	....	185	170	18	5	3	....	3	6	6	1,500	..	1	200		
Total	20		6104		6124	5474	646	262	258	170	390	65	59	$42.400	..	15	$9,450		$640 00	$2.

DELHI DISTRICT.

Monroe		2	338	....	340	321	38	12	31	10	10	1	1	3,000	..	1	2,000		
West Monroe			143	1	144	139	....	17	12	9	1	3	3	3,800	..	1	700		225 ..
Bastrop		1	123	....	124	119	2	8	5	6	1	1	1	8,000	..	1	1,500		
Lind Grove		1	267	....	268	274	9	2	17	5	6	4	4	2,150	..	1	500		25 ..
Delhi			92	....	92	74	15	8	5	....	5	1	1	900	..	1	500		
Floyd		1	276	....	277	26	14	....			8	3	3	2,770	..	1	500		
Lake Providence			83	....	83	86	....	2	5	2	..	2	2	2,300	..	1	800		50 ..
Oak Ridge			172	....	172	154	12	14	8	15	5	3	3	2,500	..	1	1,000		
Harrisonburg			129	....	129	120	11	....	2	8	4	2	2	2,000	..				75 ..
Waterproof			89	....	89	85	6	5	7	3	....	2	2	1,800	..	1	600		10 ..
Winnsboro		1	196	....	197	185	14	2	4	17	4	4	3	2,300	..				
Rayville			226	....	226	203	24	1	2	12	16	2	2	1,800	..	1	500		200 ..
Oakley and Vidalia		1	146	..	147	135	9	17	14	23	2	6	6	3,500	..	1	325		
Total	7		2280	1	2288	2158	154	88	112	110	62	36	33	$36.9 0	..	11	$8,925		$585 ..	$2.

RECAPITULATION.

New Orleans District	14	8	2992	6	3006	2935	168	219	336	195	30	17	21	221,350 00	6	22,900	....	52,450 00	4,
Shreveport "	19	11	4290	....	4301	4137	289	123	248	151	147	81	63	82.800 00	12	7,450	....	2,410 00	4,
Opelousas "	19	10	3215	1	3226	2880	337	213	209	234	79	36	24	55,670 00	11	14,960	....	1,245 10	3,
Alexandria "	16	16	3373	....	3389	8089	347	151	198	201	118	43	36	29,100 00	13	7,450	2000	3,195 00	2,
Arcadia "	17	20	6104	....	6124	5474	646	262	258	170	390	65	59	42.400 00	15	9,460	....	640 00	2,
Delhi "	13	7	2280	1	2288	2158	154	88	112	110	62	36	33	36,920 00	11	8,925	....	585 00	2,
Baton Rouge "	15	32	5736	1	5769	5335	433	159	158	230	196	67	60	43,400 00	13	10,212	1000	83,390 00	3,
Total	113	104	27990	9	28103	26028	2374	1215	1519	1291	1022	345	296	$511,640 00	81	$81,397	5000	$143,915 00	$23,
Total last year	96	86	21114	8	21208	19763	1666	871	1632	969	615		241	$468,834 00	62	$64,155	400	$147,127 00	$28,
Increase	17	18	*6876	1	*6895	6265	708	344		322	407		55	$42,806 00	19	$17,182	1000		
Decrease									113									$3,212 00	$4.

* This very large increase in membership arises from the addition of a part of the Woodville Dist., Mississippi Confe

FINANCE.

TABLE No. II.

NEW ORLEANS DISTRICT.

Column headers:

NAME OF CHARGE.	Presiding Elder		Preacher in Charge.		Bishops.		Conference Claimants.		For. Missions.		Domestic Missions.		Church Extension.		Education.		American Bible Soc'y. Paid.	Epis. Del. Gen'l Conf.	Other Objects.	Woman's For. Miss. Society.	Woman's Parsonage & Home Miss. Society.	Incidental Expenses.	Payne & Lane Inst'ts	Total from all Sources.
	Ass'd.	Paid.	Ass'd.	Paid.	Ass'd.	Paid.	Ass'd.	Paid.	Ass'd.	Paid.	Ass'd.	Paid.	Ass'd.	Paid.	Ass'd.	Paid.	Ass'd. Paid.							

New Orleans District charges
Carondelet Street, New Orleans; Felicity Street; Rayne Memorial; Louisiana Avenue; Moreau Street; Peters Avenue and Jackson Ave.; Carrollton Avenue, New Orleans; Algiers; Parker Chapel; Baton Rouge; Gretna and St. Charles Sts.; Lafayette; Donaldsonville, New Orleans; Lower Coast Missions.

BATON ROUGE DISTRICT.
Jackson; Zachary; Clinton; Bayou Sara; Wilson; Franklinton; Covington; Donaldsonville; Amite City; St. Tammany; Port Vincent; Ascension; Baton Rouge; East Baton Rouge.

OPELOUSAS DISTRICT.
Opelousas; Washington; Vermillion Bayou; Lafayette and Bayou; Abbeville; New Iberia; Franklin; Lake Charles; Jennings; Lake Arthur; Crowley; Jeanerette; Morgan City; St. Martinville.

ALEXANDRIA DISTRICT.
Alexandria; Evergreen; Lecompte; Shreveport; Melville and Big Cane; Spring Creek; Dry Creek; Montgomery; Colfax; Coushatta; Natchitoches; Boyce and DeRidder; Pineville; Bayou Chicot; Nugent Mission.

Total.

..ions.	Domestic Missions.		Church Extension.		Education.		American Bible Soc'y. Paid.	Exp. Del. Gen'l Conf.		Other Objects.	Woman's For. Miss. Society	Woman's Parsonage & Home Miss. Society.	Incidental Expenses.	Paine & Lane Inst'te.	Total from all Sources.
'aid.	Ass'd.	Paid.	Ass'd.	Paid.	Ass'd.	Paid.		Ass'd.	Paid.						
!40 ..	100 ..	100 ..	65 ..	65 ..	36 ..	36 ..	10 ..	12 50	13 50	.... ..	....		6 50		6 50	5321 96
50 ..	32 ..	30 25	22 ..	11 ..	12 ..	4 ..		4 50	2 25	.... ..					1 45	639 90
50 ..	42 ..	15 ..	26 15	10 ..	15 ..	5 ..		......	......	65 00					.. ..	830 00
95 ..	45 ..	40 ..	28 ..	20 ..	15 ..	15 ..		6 00	6 00	.... ..		34 65		110 00	2 00	1138 47
S'18 ..	20 ..	.. ..	16 50	.. ..	.. ..	6 ..		3 00	......	20 00					1 30	476 85
M 6 ..	.. ..	.. ..	.. ..	.. ..	.. ..	.. ..		......	......							93 75
Cr24 80	27 ..	5 05	17 ..	2 45	9 ..	1 40		3 00	40						30	478 90
M	10 ..	.. ..	4 75	.. ..	3 ..	.. ..		......	......							24 60
M	13 ..	.. ..	8 50	.. ..	5 ..	.. ..		......	......							148 15
Se27 40	38 ..	1 50	24 ..	8 ..	14 ..	2 ..	2 ..	5 00	......			5 00				538 40
G'39 23	30 50	.. ..	20 ..	.. ..	10 ..	.. ..		......	......							285 68
A'13 75	33 ..	5 ..	22 ..	2 ..	10 ..	2 ..	1 ..	4 51	1 00	6 00					1 00	461 90
Ci13 ..	22 ..	3 50	14 ..	2 ..	8 ..	8 ..	1 50	......	......	7 00						276 85
Pl15 ..	19 ..	2 25	12 ..	.. ..	7 ..	.. ..		2 70	......							464 50
N40 ..	33 ..	23 25	22 ..	11 ..	12 ..	4 ..	1 25	......	......							700 10
Ci25 ..	30 ..	15 ..	30 ..	10 ..	10 ..	12 ..		4 50	......							1233 50
W 5 ..	22 ..	1 50	13 80	2 ..	8 41	1 ..		3 00	......							555 50
R 9 ..	22 ..	.. ..	14 50	.. ..	8 ..	.. ..		3 50	......				....			235 85
Sc.. ..	5 50	.. ..	3 50	.. ..	2 ..	.. ..		......	......							58 00
N.. ..																
D.71 18	544 ..	242 30	363 70	143 45	190 41	90 40	15 75	53 21	23 15	98 00	39 65	6 50	110 00		12 55	13962 86
F.																

90 00	35 00	40 00	22 00	22 00	10 00	10 00	5 00	10 00	.....	25 00					7 15	1138 65
50 00	35 00	18 00	25 00	10 00	10 00	2 00		5 00	2 00						1 00	705 00
95 00	60 00	60 00	22 00	22 00	10 00	10 00		7 00	7 00			9 95			2 50	1007 45
H16 00	20 00	5 00	15 00	5 00	8 00	2 50		1 00	1 00						1 00	533 41
H 5 00	30 00	2 50	20 00	2 00	15 00	1 00	1 00	.....	.....						.. ..	390 00
M70 00	60 00	40 00	34 00	20 00	15 00	7 50		10 00	2 50						1 00	1204 88
R35 00	35 00	15 00	25 00	18 75	10 00	7 50		5 00	1 75						2 00	1521 90
S80 00	65 00	45 00	35 00	25 00	15 00	8 00		10 00	.. ..		27 60	14 50			5 00	1089 61
A10 00	30 00	.. ..	16 00	.. ..	9 00	.. ..		.....	.....						.. ..	226 00
S50 00	25 00	19 00	15 00	11 00	8 00	6 00		3 00	2 00						1 53	581 75
R 5 00	35 00	5 00	25 00	.. ..	10 00	.. ..		.....	.....						.. ..	599 50
V17 40	20 00	10 75	15 00	5 70	10 00	5 35		.....	.....						.. ..	397 70
V10 00	40 00	10 00	20 00	2 00	15 00	.. ..		.....	.....						.. ..	1265 95
D50 00	20 00	15 00	15 00	10 00	10 00	8 00		1 50	1 50				22 80		1 00	611 35
F20 00	10 00	10 00	12 00	.. ..	5 00	.. ..		1 00	.....						.. ..	657 60
T55 00	45 00	27 00	25 00	16 50	10 00	10 00	1 25	7 00	.....				35 00		2 00	1040 00
V 5 00	20 00	2 00	10 00	.. ..	10 00	.. ..		.....	5 00						.. ..	242 00
L.																
C63 40	585 00	324 25	351 00	169 95	180 00	77 85	7 25	60 50	22 75	25 00	27 60	24 45	57 80		24 15	13212 75
G																

50 ..	50 ..	50 ..	37 50	37 50	20 ..	20 ..	......	10 ..	10 ..	1866 20				4 ..	3604 90
24 ..	35 ..	9 ..	20 ..	5 ..	12 50	2 ..		5 ..	.....			79 50		......	718 95
M20 ..	30 ..	10 ..	20 ..	10 ..	10 ..	2 ..		7 ..	.....			45 ..		......	694 28
W 8 ..	30 ..	3 ..	20 ..	.. ..	10 ..	.. ..		.. ..	5 ..					......	96 00
B32 85	30 ..	22 60	30 ..	22 60	12 50	11 ..		5 ..	3 ..	291 50		13 50	3 ..	1 50	1247 10
L. ..	25 ..	8 ..	20 ..	5 ..	12 50	.. ..		5 ..	.....					......	297 89
D17 10	30 ..	3 50	30 ..	2 50	12 50	1 75	1 25	5 ..	75			35 ..		1 25	804 61
F36 95	35 ..	10 ..	30 ..	.. ..	14 ..	3 50		.. ..	.....					......	787 55
L 5 ..	25 ..	5 ..	.. ..	.. ..	.. ..	.. ..		.. ..	.....					......	382 00
O26 50	27 50	.. ..	25 ..	.. ..	10 ..	.. ..	1 65	.. ..	.....					......	475 20
H40 ..	32 50	15 ..	28 ..	15 ..	12 50	2 50		.. ..	.....	71 27				......	872 03
W 8 ..	15 ..	3 ..	12 50	2 ..	5 ..	50		.. ..	.....					......	260 25
V 5 ..	30 ..	1 50	25 ..	1 ..	12 50	1 ..		5 ..	.....	25 ..				......	510 75
B															
O3 40	395 ..	140 60	298 ..	100 60	144 ..	44 25	2 90	42 ..	13 75	2258 97	....	13 50	162 50	6 75	10751 51

22 17	800 90	558 05	594 00	440 38	275 00	198 18	307 15	92 00	79 25	3956 49	653 46	205 45	3210 78	25 06	29248 35
N'1 18	544 00	242 30	363 70	143 45	190 41	90 40	15 75	53 21	23 15	98 00	39 65	6 50	110 00	12 55	13962 86
S'37 20	470 05	227 35	358 45	162 80	139 15	59 00	8 05	23 50	6 75	1102 46	128 55	113 30	301 72	9 50	16437 76
G'51 90	235 40	93 75	179 55	44 29	65 50	16 15	1 00	5 60	2 05	222 75	10 00	14 45	82 80	2 0.	8b17 68
A33 40	585 00	324 25	351 00	169 95	180 00	77 85	7 25	60 50	22 75	25 00	27 60	24 45	57 80	24 15	13212 75
A'13 40	395 00	140 60	298 00	100 60	144 00	44 25	2 90	42 00	13 75	2258 97		13 50	162 50	6 75	10751 51
T'78 30	374 56	228 40	247 00	128 10	155 00	88 50	2 15	.. ..	.....	1849 45	29 40		74 35	......	13072 85
E															
37 55	3404 01	1814 70	2391 70	1189 57	1149 06	574 33	344 25	276 81	147 70	9013 12	888 66	377 65	3999 90	80 01	105503 76
58 67	2845 30	1545 71	1947 90	1016 01	972 25	509 05	397 05	.....	11 30	4184 84*	523 97	182 15	2021 33	77 80	92408 70
98 88	558 71	268 99	443 80	173 56	176 81	65 28	......	......	136 40	4828 28	364 69	195 50	1978 57	2 21	13095 06
......	......	......	......	......	......		52 80								

..e compared with last year.

NEW ORLEANS DISTRICT.

NAME OF CHARGE.	No. of Epworth Leagues.	No. of Epworth League Members.	No. of Schools.	No. of Officers and Teachers.	No. of Scholars.	Amount Collected for Sunday Schools.	Amount Collected for Missions.	Amount Collected on Children's Day.	Amount Collected for Other Objects.	Money Raised by Epworth League.	Total Amount Raised.
Carondelet St., New Orleans.	1	80	2·	32	275	260 00	* 119 80	17 25	....	35 90	415 70
Felicity Street, " "	1	67	2	31	203	109 00	61 06	9 35	25 00	....	204 41
Rayne Memorial, " "	1	29	1	24	185	....	133 72	31 35	95 80	....	260 87
Louisiana Ave., " "	1	40	2	35	335	163 69	70 00	15 65	....	39 00	288 34
Moreau Street, " "	1	44	2	19	228	138 00	12 33	3 75	....	....	204 08
Carrollton Ave., " "	.....	.....	1	15	116	130 41	... ..	... ..	....	....	130 41
Gretna & Craps St. " "	1	23	2	13	105	100 00	... ..	... ..	....	....	100 00
Parker Chapel, " "	1	38	1	19	175	89 15	38 25	5 25	....	16 75	149 40
Dryades Street, " "	.....	.....	1	13	85	81 41	18 39	3 15	....	....	102 95
Algiers " "	.....	.....	2	22	177	65 88	84 78	22 34	100 75	....	273 75
Plaquemine & Donaldsonville.	.....	.....	4	21	137	80 00	10 00	... ..	....	....	90 00
Baton Rouge....	.....	.....	4	42	235	150 48	56 48	16 90	....	....	223 86
Gross Tete and False River..	.....	.....	1	3	24	10 00	... ..	... ..	....	....	10 00
Lower Coast Mission....	.....	.....	2	12	65	4 60	... ..	... ..	....	....	4 60
Total.................	7	321	27	301	2345	$1382 62	$604 81	$124 99	$221 55	$91 65	$2458 37

* Of this amount $73.53 is included in Finance Table.

BATON ROUGE DISTRICT.

NAME OF CHARGE.	No. of Epworth Leagues.	No. of Epworth League Members.	No. of Schools.	No. of Officers and Teachers.	No. of Scholars.	Amount Collected for Sunday Schools.	Amount Collected for Missions.	Amount Collected on Children's Day.	Amount Collected for Other Objects.	Money Raised by Epworth League.	Total Amount Raised.
Jackson................			1	14	150	38 55	....	....	20	....	38 75
Zachary...			1	7	55	16 00	....	....	20 00	....	36 00
Bayou Sara			7	35	250	.. ..	....	....	....	....	.. ..
Wilson...................			3	19	160	18 00	....	....	....	....	18 00
Franklinton.............			5	24	165	25 60	....	....	5 00	....	30 45
Covington...............			2	8	63	20 00	....	6 70	....	....	26 70
Ponchatoula.............			4	15	195	33 25	....	6 60	....	....	39 85
Live Oak...............			6	20	159	13 80	....	6 25	....	....	20 15
Talisheek..............			4	12	75	10 00	....	....	7 00	....	17 00
E. Feliciana...			8	15	200	25 00	....	....	....	....	25 00
St. Helena..............			6	24	180	21 00	....	....	....	....	21 00
Port Vincent..........;			3	15	105	11 50	1 35	2 50	17 10	....	32 45
Amite City..............			4	25	165	43 00	....	11 00	....	....	54 00
Clinton.................			1	13	132	16 78	3 00	....	....	....	19 78
E. Baton Rouge..........			3	12	70	12 00	....	....	....	....	12 00
Total.................			58	258	2034	303 88	$4 35	$33 05	$49 30	....	$391 13

OPELOUSAS DISTRICT.

NAME OF CHARGE.	No. of Epworth Leagues.	No. of Epworth League Members.	No. of Schools.	No. of Officers and Teachers.	No. of Scholars.	Amount Collected for Sunday Schools.	Amount Collected for Missions.	Amount Collected on Children's Day.	Amount Collected for Other Objects.	Money Raised by Epworth League.	Total Amount Raised.
Opelousas................			3	26	145	70 00	....	5 00	....	....	75 00
Washington.......			2	9	50	14 35	....	....	....	....	14 35
Plaquemine Brulé			5	25	201	25 00	5 25	....	2 00	....	32 25
Lafayette and Rayne			2	19	144	54 15	....	10 70	....	....	64 85
Crowley.................			1	17	186	65 00	10 00	6 50	....	....	81 50
Abbeville................			3	30	150	30 00	....	....	....	....	30 00
New Iberia..............			1	16	107	74 00	17 15	....	....	....	91 15
Franklin................			1	6	75	19 00	....	4 00	....	....	23 00
Lake Charles—Broad St			1	16	236	92 71	....	8 27	....	....	100 98
" " —Jackson St....	2	24	3	18	150	32 00	12 00	....	....	....	44 00
Pattersonville..........			1	10	63	20 00	....	....	....	....	20 00
Sulphur Mine............			1	4	23	4 50	....	....	....	....	4 50
Grand Cheniere.....,.......	1	27	3	18	117	43 90	....	....	....	7 20	51 10
Indian Bayou............			5	48	375	80 00	....	1 50	....	....	82 40
Lake Arthur..............			3	20	130	30 00	....	3 60	....	....	33 60
Jeanerette..............			1	10	50	29 00	....	5 00	....	....	34 00
Morgan City............			2	25	145	75 00	....	....	....	....	75 00
St. Martinsville.........			1	4	22	6 85	....	....	....	....	6 85
Total.................	3	51	39	321	2368	766 36	$44 40	44 57	2 00	$7 20	$864 53

ALEXANDRIA DISTRICT.

NAME OF CHARGE.	No. of Epworth Leagues.	No. of Epworth League Members.	No. of Schools.	No. of Officers and Teachers.	No. of Scholars.	Amount Collected for Sunday Schools.	Amount Collected for Missions.	Amount Collected on Children's Day.	Amount Collected for Other Objects.	Money Raised by Epworth League.	Total Amount Raised.
Alexandria...........			1	8	94	23 54	....	....	....	....	23 54
Evergreen................			3	12	100	17 00	....	....	....	....	17 00
Lecompte & White Chapel.....			3	16	100	50 00	5 75	....	....	....	55 75
Simmsport...............			4	16	80	4 80	....	....	....	....	4 80
Melville and Big Cane			2	8	60	30 00	....	....	....	....	30 00
Spring Creek.............			3	15	135	6 00	....	....	....	....	6 00
Dry Creek...............			2	12	105	15 50	....	....	....	....	15 50
Montgomery..............			3	13	93	7 25	....	....	....	....	7 25
Ada.....................			3	12	40	5 00	....	....	....	....	5 00
Centreville.............			1	6	40	4 45	5 90	....	....	....	10 35
Columbia................			3	26	75	.. ..	....	....	....	....	.. ..
Boyce and Colfax.........			3	15	140	25 00	....	....	....	....	25 00
Pineville................			6	30	200	10 00	5 00	....	....	....	15 00
Bayou Chicot.............			4	16	120	12 00	....	....	....	....	12 00
Nugent Mission...........			3	10	104	20 00	....	....	....	....	20 00
Total.................			44	215	1486	$230 54	$16 65	....	....	....	$247 19

Table No. II.

FINANCE.

SHREVEPORT DISTRICT.

NAME OF CHARGE.	Presiding Elder.		Preacher in Charge.		Bishops.		Conference Claimants.		For. Missions.		Domestic Missions.		Church Extension.		Education.		American Bible Soc'y.		Sup. Del. Gen'l Conf.		Other Objects.		Woman's For. Mis. Society.		Woman's Parsonage & Home Mission Society.		Incidental Expenses.		Total from all Sources.	Paid to Last Conf'ce.
	Ass'd.	Paid.	Ass'd.	Paid.	Ass'd.	Paid.	Ass'd.	Paid.	Ass'd.	Paid.	Ass'd.	Paid.	Ass'd.	Paid.	Ass'd.	Paid.	Ass'd.	Paid.	Ass'd.	Paid.	Ass'd.	Paid.								

Shreveport—First Church and City ...

ARCADIA DISTRICT.

DELHI DISTRICT.

RECAPITULATION.

* This amount includes funds for relief of poor, which not being reported separately this year cannot be compared with last year.

Epworth Leagues and Sunday Schools.

NEW ORLEANS DISTRICT.

NAME OF CHARGE.	No. of Epworth Leagues.	No. of Epworth League Members.	No. of Schools.	No. of Officers and Teachers.	No. of Scholars.	Amount Collected for Sunday Schools.	Amount Collected for Missions.	Amount Collected on Children's Day.	Amount Collected for Other Objects.	Money Raised by Epworth League.	Total Amount Raised.
Carondelet St., New Orleans.	1	80	2	32	275	260 00	*119 80	17 25	....	35 90	415 70
Felicity Street, " "	1	67	2	31	203	109 00	61 06	9 35	25 00	....	204 41
Rayne Memorial, " "	1	29	1	24	185	......	133 72	31 35	95 80	....	260 87
Louisiana Ave., " "	1	40	2	35	335	163 69	70 00	15 65	....	39 00	288 34
Moreau Street, " "	1	44	2	19	228	138 00	12 33	3 75	....	......	204 08
Carrollton Ave., " "	......	......	1	15	116	130 41	......	......	......	......	130 41
Gretna & Craps St. "	1	23	2	13	105	100 00	......	......	......	......	100 00
Parker Chapel, " "	1	38	1	19	175	89 15	38 25	5 25	......	16 75	149 40
Dryades Street, " "	......	......	1	13	85	81 41	18 39	3 15	......	......	102 95
Algiers " "	......	......	2	22	177	65 88	84 78	22 34	100 75	......	273 75
Plaquemine & Donaldsonville.	......	......	4	21	137	80 00	10 00	......	......	......	90 00
Baton Rouge..........	......	......	4	42	235	150 48	56 48	16 90	......	......	223 86
Gross Tete and False River...	......	......	1	3	24	10 00	......	......	......	......	10 00
Lower Coast Mission....	......	......	2	12	65	4 60	......	......	......	......	4 60
Total...................	7	321	27	301	2345	$1382 62	$604 81	$124 99	$221 55	$91 65	$2458 37

* Of this amount $73.53 is included in Finance Table.

BATON ROUGE DISTRICT.

NAME OF CHARGE.	No. of Epworth Leagues.	No. of Epworth League Members.	No. of Schools.	No. of Officers and Teachers.	No. of Scholars.	Amount Collected for Sunday Schools.	Amount Collected for Missions.	Amount Collected on Children's Day.	Amount Collected for Other Objects.	Money Raised by Epworth League.	Total Amount Raised.
Jackson..........	......	......	1	14	150	38 55	......	......	20	......	38 75
Zachary....	......	......	1	7	55	16 00	......	......	20 00	......	36 00
Bayou Sara..........	......	......	7	35	250	......	......	......	......	......	......
Wilson..........	......	......	3	19	160	18 00	......	......	......	......	18 00
Franklinton..........	......	......	5	24	165	25 60	......	......	5 00	......	30 45
Covington..........	......	......	2	8	63	20 00	......	6 70	......	......	26 70
Ponchatoula..........	......	......	4	15	195	33 25	......	6 60	......	......	39 85
Live Oak..........	......	......	6	20	159	13 80	......	6 25	......	......	20 15
Talisheek..........	......	......	4	12	75	10 00	......	......	7 00	......	17 00
E. Feliciana..........	......	......	8	15	200	25 00	......	......	......	......	25 00
St. Helena..........	......	......	6	24	180	21 00	......	......	......	......	21 00
Port Vincent..........	......	......	3	15	105	11 50	1 35	2 50	17 10	......	32 45
Amite City..........	......	......	4	25	165	43 00	......	11 00	......	......	54 00
Clinton..........	......	......	1	13	132	16 78	3 00	......	......	......	19 78
E. Baton Rouge..........	......	......	3	12	70	12 00	......	......	......	......	12 00
Total...................	......	......	58	258	2034	303 88	$4 35	$33 05	$49 30	......	$391 13

OPELOUSAS DISTRICT.

NAME OF CHARGE.	No. of Epworth Leagues.	No. of Epworth League Members.	No. of Schools.	No. of Officers and Teachers.	No. of Scholars.	Amount Collected for Sunday Schools.	Amount Collected for Missions.	Amount Collected on Children's Day.	Amount Collected for Other Objects.	Money Raised by Epworth League.	Total Amount Raised.
Opelousas..........	......	......	3	26	145	70 00	......	5 00	......	......	75 00
Washington.....	......	......	2	9	50	14 35	......	......	......	......	14 35
Plaquemine Brulé..	......	......	5	25	201	25 00	5 25	......	2 00	......	32 25
Lafayette and Rayne..........	......	......	2	19	144	54 15	......	10 70	......	......	64 85
Crowley..........	......	......	1	17	156	65 00	10 00	6 50	......	......	81 50
Abbeville..........	......	......	3	30	150	30 00	......	......	......	......	30 00
New Iberia..........	......	......	1	16	107	74 00	17 15	......	......	......	91 15
Franklin..........	......	......	1	6	75	19 00	......	4 00	......	......	23 00
Lake Charles—Broad St ...	......	......	1	16	236	92 71	......	8 27	......	......	100 98
" " —Jackson St....	2	24	3	18	150	32 00	12 00	......	......	......	44 00
Pattersonville..........	......	......	1	10	63	20 00	......	......	......	......	20 00
Sulphur Mine..........	......	......	1	4	22	4 50	......	......	......	......	4 50
Grand Cheniere....	1	27	3	18	117	43 90	......	......	......	7 20	51 10
Indian Bayou..........	......	......	5	48	375	80 90	......	1 50	......	......	82 40
Lake Arthur..........	......	......	3	20	130	30 00	......	3 60	......	......	33 60
Jeanerette..........	......	......	1	10	50	29 00	......	5 00	......	......	34 00
Morgan City..........	......	......	2	25	145	75 00	......	......	......	......	75 00
St. Martinsville..........	......	......	1	4	22	6 85	......	......	......	......	6 85
Total.................	3	51	39	321	2368	766 36	$44 40	44 57	2 00	$7 20	$864 53

ALEXANDRIA DISTRICT.

NAME OF CHARGE.	No. of Epworth Leagues.	No. of Epworth League Members.	No. of Schools.	No. of Officers and Teachers.	No. of Scholars.	Amount Collected for Sunday Schools.	Amount Collected for Missions.	Amount Collected on Children's Day.	Amount Collected for Other Objects.	Money Raised by Epworth League.	Total Amount Raised.
Alexandria..........	......	......	1	8	94	23 54	......	......	......	......	23 54
Evergreen..........	......	......	3	12	100	17 00	......	......	......	......	17 00
Lecompte & White Chapel.....	......	......	3	16	100	50 00	5 75	......	......	......	55 75
Simmsport..........	......	......	4	16	80	4 80	......	......	......	......	4 80
Melville and Big Cane	......	......	2	8	60	30 00	......	......	......	......	30 00
Spring Creek..........	......	......	3	15	135	6 00	......	......	......	......	6 00
Dry Creek..........	......	......	2	12	105	15 50	......	......	......	......	15 50
Montgomery.......	......	......	3	13	93	7 25	......	......	......	......	7 25
Ada.......	......	......	3	12	40	5 00	......	......	......	......	5 00
Centreville..........	......	......	1	6	40	4 45	5 90	......	......	......	10 35
Columbia..........	......	......	3	26	75	......	......	......	......	......	......
Boyce and Colfax..........	......	......	3	15	140	25 00	......	......	......	......	25 00
Pineville..........	......	......	6	30	200	10 00	5 00	......	......	......	15 00
Bayou Chicot..........	......	......	4	16	120	12 00	......	......	......	......	12 00
Nugent Mission..........	......	......	3	10	104	20 00	......	......	......	......	20 00
Total...................	......	......	44	215	1486	$230 54	$16 65	......	......	......	$247 19

SHREVEPORT DISTRICT.

NAME OF CHARGE.	No. of Epworth Leagues.	No. of Epworth League Members.	No. of Schools.	No. of Officers and Teachers.	No. of Scholars.	Amount Collected for Sunday Schools.	Amount Collected for Missions.	Amount Collected on Children's Day.	Amount Collected for Other Objects.	Amount Raised by Epworth League.	Total Amount Raised.
Shreveport— First Church and City Mission........... ...	2	61	2	22	216	243 00	9 90	....	....	....	252
Mooringsport.	....	....	1	6	59	9 00	....	....	5 00	....	14
Caddo................	....	....	4	32	160	40 00	....	....	17 25	....	57
Mansfield............	1	20	2	16	110	38 20	....	....	....	5 00	43
Many.................	1	12	3	17	120	10 00	....	....	....	....	10
Sabine................	....	....	2	20	60	20 00	....	....	....	....	20
Grand Cane...........	....	....	3	13	100	12 50	....	....	....	....	19
Anacoco and S. Vernon.	....	....	5	15	75	....	....	....	6 75	....	....
Cane River........	....	....	1	5	27	....	....	....	....	....	....
Pleasant Hill...........	....	....	3	30	273	70 00	3 60	80	240 00	....	314
Natchitoches *	....	....	....	....	....	....	....	....	....	....	....
Coushatta.	....	....	2	9	60	11 05	2 75	....	....	....	13
Wesley	....	....	5	17	122	3 85	....	....	....	....	....
Red River...........	....	....	1	6	12	1 80	....	....	....	....	1
South Bossier.........	....	....	4	20	100	20 00	....	....	20 00	....	40
North "	....	....	7	43	236	12 39	....	....	....	....	12
DeSoto.................	....	....	3	15	75	12 00	....	....	....	....	12
Fort Jessup.........	....	....	3	18	150	8 00	....	....	....	....	8
Victoria & W. Natchitoches....	....	....	2	8	49	9 00	....	....	....	....	9
Total.......	4	93	53	312	2009	$520 79	$16 25	$49 80	$245 00	....	$827

* No report.

ARCADIA DISTRICT.

NAME OF CHARGE.	No. of Epworth Leagues.	No. of Epworth League Members.	No. of Schools.	No. of Officers and Teachers.	No. of Scholars.	Amount Collected for Sunday Schools.	Amount Collected for Missions.	Amount Collected on Children's Day.	Amount Collected for Other Objects.	Amount Raised by Epworth League.	Total Amount Raised.
Homer...........................	1	51	1	12	135	27 15	4 90	3 15	....	....	35
Haynesville..................	....	....	5	30	160	17 50	....	1 20	....	....	18
Minden.......................	....	....	2	13	140	43 30	8 00	....	....	....	51
Ringgold...................	....	....	1	4	35	4 00	....	....	....	....	4
Sparta......................	....	....	5	25	300	12 00	....	....	....	....	12
Arcadia.....................	....	....	4	30	272	43 88	....	1 50	....	....	45
Summerfield..................	....	....	3	22	191	21 20	....	8 70	....	....	29
Ruston.......................	....	....	2	21	215	16 00	....	8 70	....	....	24
Vienna.......................	....	....	....	....	....	....	....	....	....	....	....
Vernon and Gainesville......	....	....	1	12	40	12 00	....	4 25	....	....	16
Downsville '.................	....	....	5	30	160	17 50	....	3 00	....	....	20
Farmerville.................	....	....	2	8	66	30 45	....	7 55	....	....	38
Calhoun and La Pine........	....	....	4	18	120	27 00	....	....	....	....	34
Tulip.......................	....	....	4	16	154	13 55	1 50	5 00	....	....	20
Valley.......................	....	....	2	10	60	7 50	....	12 00	....	....	7
Lisbon......................	2	150	3	25	198	25 00	6 75	....	....	....	43
Gannsville...................	....	....	....	....	....	....	....	....	....	....	....
Total...................	3	201	44	276	2246	$318 03	$21 15	$55 05	....	....	$40

DELHI

NAME OF CHARGE.	No. of Epworth Leagues.	No. of Epworth League Members.	No. of Schools.	No. of Officers and Teachers.	No. of Scholars.	Amount Collected for Sunday Schools.	Amount Collected for Missions.	Amount Collected on Children's Day.	Amount Collected for Other Objects.	Amount Raised by Epworth League.	Total Amount Raised.
Monroe.......................	....	....	1	16	153	72 20	15 00	....	....	....	87
West Monroe.................	....	....	2	14	94	26 75	4 75	4 25	....	....	35
Bastrop......................	....	....	1	8	40	12 00	....	....	....	....	12
Lind Grove..................	....	....	5	20	116	11 00	....	....	....	....	11
Delhi........................	....	....	1	7	61	17 60	....	....	....	....	17
Floyd........................	....	....	1	7	35	4 00	....	....	....	....	4
Lake Providence.............	....	....	1	7	64	12 50	12 55	5 60	3 00	....	33
Oak Ridge...................	....	....	3	22	114	13 00	....	12 25	....	....	25
Harrisonburg.................	....	....	1	8	60	6 00	....	9 75	....	....	15
Waterproof..................	1	34	1	6	45	21 50	4 70	5 70	....	....	21
Rayville.....................	....	....	2	10	80	19 00	....	3 30	....	....	22
Oakley and Vidalia..........	....	....	2	9	56	3 10	....	....	....	....	3
Winnsboro...................	....	....	4	18	120	27 00	....	4 25	3 00	....	34
Total.......	1	34	25	152	1038	$235 65	$37 00	$45 10	$6 00	....	$32

RECAPITULAT

	No. of Epworth Leagues.	No. of Epworth League Members.	No. of Schools.	No. of Officers and Teachers.	No. of Scholars.	Amount Collected for Sunday Schools.	Amount Collected for Missions.	Amount Collected on Children's Day.	Amount Collected for Other Objects.	Amount Raised by Epworth League.	Total Amount Raised.
New Orleans District.........	7	321	27	301	2345	$1382 62	$604 81	$124 99	$221 55	$91 65	$2458
Shreveport "	4	93	53	312	2009	520 79	16 25	49 80	245 00	....	827
Opelousas "	3	51	39	321	2368	766 36	44 40	44 57	2 00	7 20	864
Alexandria "	....	....	44	215	1486	230 54	16 65	....	....	....	247
Arcadia "	3	201	44	276	2246	318 03	21 15	55 05	....	....	401
Delhi "	1	34	25	152	1038	235 65	37 00	45 10	6 00	....	323
Baton Rouge "	....	....	58	258	2034	303 88	4 35	33 05	49 30	....	391
Total.....	18	700	290	1835	13526	$3757 87	$744 61	$352 56	$523 85	$98 85	$551
Total last year...........	....	196	1341	10251	....	$3583 60	$957 31	$217 01	$516 54	$83 30	$52
Increase.....	*18	700	94	494	3275	$154 27	....	$135 55	$7 31	$15 55	$22
Decrease...	....	....	....	....	....	....	$212 70	....	....	....	....

* There were several Lea..an accurate comparison cannot be mad

CPSIA information can be obtained
at www.ICGtesting.com
Printed in the USA
BVHW04*1018300818
526054BV00005B/76/P